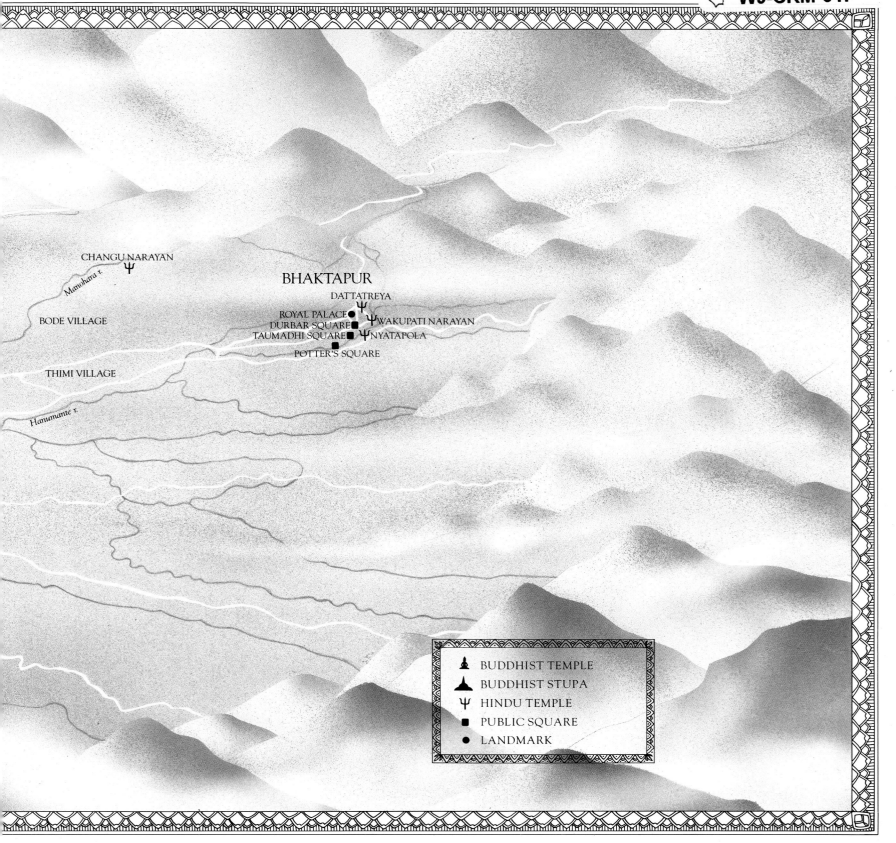

CHANGU NARAYAN Ψ

Manohara r.

BODE VILLAGE

BHAKTAPUR

DATTATREYA Ψ

ROYAL PALACE ●
DURBAR SQUARE ■ Ψ WAKUPATI NARAYAN
TAUMADHI SQUARE ■ Ψ NYATAPOLA
POTTER'S SQUARE ■

THIMI VILLAGE

Hanumante r.

🛕	BUDDHIST TEMPLE
▲	BUDDHIST STUPA
Ψ	HINDU TEMPLE
■	PUBLIC SQUARE
●	LANDMARK

KATHMANDU

KATHMANDU
City on the Edge of the World

PHOTOGRAPHS BY Thomas L. Kelly

TEXT BY Patricia Roberts

ABBEVILLE PRESS • PUBLISHERS • NEW YORK

To the Nepalese people, who continue to live out

the Kathmandu Valley's rich traditions.

JACKET FRONT

Kathmandu's urban sprawl engulfs the Hindu temples that outline the main palace and Durbar Square. The city is home to a melange of people and cultures found nowhere else on earth.

JACKET BACK

A Hindu ascetic, or Sadhu.

HALF-TITLE PAGE

Uma-Mahesvara stone statue, Parphing.

FIRST SPREAD

Carrying his trident, Shiva's weapon, Pagali-nanda Baba walks through the Pashupatinath forest after meditations.

SECOND SPREAD

Seen from Nagarkot, the full moon illuminates Nepal's Himalayan range.

THIRD SPREAD

A young Nepali girl weeds a mustard field. The crop is grown for the cluster of basal leaves that are used as greens, and also for the seeds, which are pressed for cooking oil.

FACING TITLE PAGE

Silhouetted Narayan temple built by Jung Bahadur Kunwar Rana, mastermind behind the overthrow of the Shahs.

EDITOR: Alan Axelrod
DESIGNER: Nai Y. Chang
COPY CHIEF: Robin James
PRODUCTION MANAGER: Dana Cole

First edition

Published in the United States of America by Abbeville Press, Inc.

Library of Congress Cataloging-in-Publication Data

Kelly, Thomas L.
    Kathmandu : city on the edge of the world / photographs by Thomas
L. Kelly ; text by Patricia Roberts.
        p.   cm.
    Includes index.
    ISBN 0-89659-960-4 : $49.95
    1. Kathmandu (Nepal)—Description—Views.   2. Kathmandu (Nepal)—Description.   3. Kathmandu (Nepal)—History.   4. Kathmandu (Nepal)—History—Pictorial works.   I. Roberts, Patricia, 1946–   .
II. Title.
DS495.8.K3K45   1989
954.96—dc20
89-14862
CIP

CONTENTS

PRELUDE

A SEPARATE REALITY

It is as if the gods uprooted a mountain. The Kathmandu Valley is a vast green space scooped from a colossal sculpture garden of jagged whites and grays. Here the snow-capped peaks of the Nepal Himalaya plunge from 29,000 to 4,400 feet, forming two hundred square miles of lush land, a palette of brilliant greens and golds overlapping in gentle terraces, a rich tapestry of croplands threaded with rivers and patched with clusters of brown-thatched houses. A city sprawls across the central quarter of the landscape, fanciful shapes rising from its low skyline of linear browns. The sun glints from gilded copper on tiered pagoda roofs. Giant carved figures, the Buddhist stupas of Swayambhu and Bodhnath, gaze with serene lotus eyes from the eastern and western edges.

Kathmandu, capital of the Kingdom of Nepal, is a merger of three ancient kingdoms. Sometimes city, sometimes village, it is in some ways a boom town groping for a new identity, in some ways a primitive land resisting change. In all ways, it is exotic, mysterious, and fascinating.

Kathmandu. The name evokes images of a fertile Shangri-la, the ultimate destination of runaways and dropouts, a Never-Never Land where time stands still. Kathmandu is the florid realm of exotica that inspired Rudyard Kipling to write, "And the wildest dreams of Kew are but the facts of Kathmandu." It is the hard K of hard rock in Bob Seeger's K-K-K-K-K-K-Kay Kat-Man-Do. It is a separate reality, an isolated land where ways of thinking are as different from those of the West as light from darkness, a confirmation that the twain, indeed, never shall meet.

Until the middle of the twentieth century, the isolation of the Kathmandu Valley took two forms, geographic and political. This shaped the traditions within the valley and preserved them from the ancient past into the present. The fertile valley is wedged between two geographical extremes, the high frozen peaks

Thatched-roof, mud-masonry houses perch among terraced fields of budding mustard plants in view of Ganesh Himal, Nagarkot.

The Himalayan mountain chain caressed by the
light of the setting sun.

of the Himalaya and the low tropical plains of northern India. The mountains and jungle isolated Kathmandu as surely as if it were an island in the sea. But just as ships navigate the sea, the men of Nepal, Tibet, and India have always traversed the mountains on footpaths.

Since 500 B.C., a major trading route has crossed the Kathmandu Valley, used by Himalayan and Indian traders to exchange goods from the outer world for Kathmandu's bountiful agricultural and artistic produce. Traders, explorers, adventurers, scholars, and holy men often lingered in the valley long months, awaiting the end of the cold Tibetan winter or the hot Indian summer. Their contrasting ideas, philosophies, and gods mingled, merged, and forged the separate reality that is Kathmandu.

Kathmandu functions according to its own measure of time. As the 1990s begin in most of the world, the Nepali calendar of Kathmandu enters into the 2050s. The religions of Kathmandu are practiced in ways unlike anywhere on earth. Here is a mosaic of Hinduism, Buddhism, tantrism, and animism, and countless additional traditions. Kathmandu's people are an ethnic mix representing four major castes and thirty-six sub-castes and speaking a commensurate number of dialects.

Kumari, a Tamang-caste girl, stares from her window. Tamang—whose name means horseman—migrated from Tibet; they are Buddhists and have settled on the marginal land surrounding the Kathmandu Valley.

A Bhaktapur Newar Jyapu farmer carries home a balanced load of wheat stalk used for mulch and cooking fuel. The bamboo pole has been a vehicle of load transport for centuries; it allows the porter to shift weight readily from one shoulder to the other as he trots down the road.

15

Newar Jyapu girl with a red bindi blessing on her forehead.

Hindu Chhetri girl.

ing four major castes and thirty-six sub-castes and speaking a commensurate number of dialects.

Until 1951, a policy of political isolation reinforced Nepal's geographic barriers. Except for a few European dignitaries, no visitors from the West were allowed into Nepal. Today, Kathmandu is open to the world. And the world has come, via international air service and highways across the mountains. Wave upon wave of outsiders have arrived, bringing foreign-aid money, projects, and new ideas that have superimposed as much change in four decades as in so many centuries of the past.

The 1950s brought Nepal's capital city to international attention when Sir Edmund Hillary and Tenzing Norgay first scaled Mount Everest, just a hundred miles to the northeast. The 1960s gave Kathmandu a new image in the Western mind: a quirky, turned on, tuned in, dropped out capital of hippieland. In the 1970s, the first scheduled international flights began to arrive—the birth of a thriving tourist industry that now brings a quarter million visitors to Kathmandu each year.

As Kathmandu enters the 1990s, it still retains its distinctive character, an ability to absorb the new without discarding the old. It is a city with growing pains, its population having jumped from 300,000 in 1950 to more than a million in the late 1980s, and expected to triple again by the year 2000.

The Kathmandu Valley is still primarily an agricultural land. The climate is mild, with a temperature seldom climbing above 86 degrees Fahrenheit or below 50 degrees. The land is rich, yielding three abundant crops of rice, wheat, mustard, and vegetables each year. The land is still best understood by taking the pace of the footpaths that wind through it and up into the surrounding mountains, where more than half of Nepal's seventeen million residents live, relying on the valley for many staples of life. Footpaths are still the lifelines; porters still walk along them on schedules as rigid as those of the interstate trucking industry. The ancient trade route of the Himalaya still stretches across the valley from east to west, and a leisurely walk along it is a journey through twenty-five centuries, through urban, village, and agricultural scenes adorned with a wealth of art and architecture.

From the valley's eastern edge, the land ripples downward, a sea of terraced ripe rice glowing gold in the strong autumn sunshine, the plants drooping with the weight of their own abundance. Harvest time presents a scene of exquisite simplicity. Workers move across the fields in steady rhythm, men in short brown pants, women in colorful cotton sarongs, cutting and threshing the grain, scooping it into burlap bags to be carried home.

Newar villages huddle on the landscape, clusters of upright brown thatched houses, home to the people who have inhabited the valley since prehistory and who still comprise half of the population. In times past, Newaris created most of the valley's greatest artworks and dominated some of its most colorful legends. Today, while they continue to create significant art, they wield little power in government, but great influence over culture. In villages and cities, they live in cooperative neighborhood units called guthis, observing age-old traditions. Neighbor helps neighbor, whether it is with the work of harvest, the glad celebrations of life, or the sad rituals of death.

The elaborate sculpting of wooden window frames and temple struts reveals the artistic prowess of the Newars, while a more prosaic aspect of life is evidenced by pumpkin and squash vines winding up walls and onto roofs, bundles of garlic and corn hanging to dry from the eaves. Streets throb with life, both human and animal. Shopkeepers sell bright bolts of cloth. Clusters of women gather around community water pumps, bathing or beating and wringing laundry, scrubbing copper cooking pots, filling tall brass water pots. Mothers nurse half-naked babies on front stoops. Chickens, ducks, goats, and pigs wander free.

Ancient is a word easy to overuse in the Kathmandu Valley, so often, and so aptly, does it apply to buildings and people. Past and present are often juxtaposed. At a roadside, a stone slab the size of tombstone, carved in ancient script, commemorates some event of distant centuries, while the red sign emblazoned across a shop wall invites the passerby to ENJOY COCA-COLA.

Religious shrines are as familiar to the landscape as McDonald's on an American highway, evidence that the gods are in control here now, as always. The valley is dotted with some three thousand Hindu and Buddhist temples and

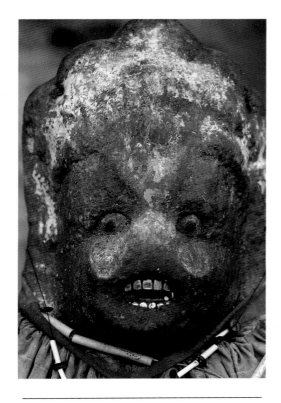

The monkey god, Hanuman.

17

religious monuments, seven of which merit mention on UNESCO's World Heritage list.

Both Hinduism and Buddhism were transported from India, though Buddhism gradually became more associated with countries to the north of Nepal. The simultaneous practice of the two religions, as well as multiple forms of tantrism and animism, shaped the valley's art, architecture, and politics. The art portrays the history of the thousands of gods that make up the Hindu pantheon, as well as the benevolent and malevolent images of Buddhism, and the erotic scenes of Hindu and Buddhist tantrism. There are countless Hindu shrines, small and large, adorned with sculpted stone gods and goddesses, smeared with vermilion powder and strewn with flower petals and bits of rice that are part of rigorous daily worship. Here and there stands that most primordial of religious symbols, the Shiva lingam, an erect phallus shape perched on a yoni, a symbolic womb.

As you move into Kathmandu City there is rarely so much as a signpost for guidance on the narrow, haphazardly winding streets. To locate a specific address, you must simply know where you are going, and if you do not, you must rely on such landmarks as a certain temple, cow pasture, or colored gate. To add to the

Superbly carved struts showing deities with their consorts, and erotic art on a corner of the Basantapur tower in Hanuman Dhoka Durbar.

confusion, street names often change every few hundred feet, designating various tols, old Newari neighborhoods, each comprised of a hundred or so houses laid out around templed squares. Traditionally, the inhabitants of each tol are of a particular caste that dictated and denoted their primary occupation: "carpenter tol," "butcher tol," "businessman tol."

In Kathmandu City all eras find a meeting place, sometimes comfortably harmonious, sometimes strangely discordant. Asphalt streets dead-end onto dirt footpaths. Houses modern enough to fit into any city's suburbia stand alongside houses of thatched roofs and mud walls, cracking and sagging with age. Sacred cows wander loose, choosing to sleep at the intersections of busy streets, turning the traffic to chaos. Electric wires drape across the ornate facades of ancient temples. The most visible sign of the present is the palace of Nepal's ruling monarch, King Birendra Bir Bikram Shah Dev. Kings have always ruled Nepal from the medieval kingdoms of the Kathmandu Valley. Each of the valley's three major kingdoms, Kathmandu, Patan, and Bhaktapur, was once a walled city with a Durbar Square at its heart, a complex of palaces and temples built to house both kings and gods. Today, these durbar squares remain the valley's most vital showcases of art, history, and worship, but Nepal's king now lives in the new Royal Palace, a half-mile north of Kathmandu's Durbar Square. It is a giant orange-and-green structure streamlined enough to be a modern railway station, only its modified pagoda roof paying homage to the past. The land that surrounds it exceeds the ten acres of the traditional Durbar Square but, unlike it, is not a chaos of temples and people; it is a quiet, isolated compound behind guarded walls.

The widest, straightest, most Westernized street of the city, Durbar Marg (Palace Road), dead-ends at the front gate of the Royal Palace. Here are sidewalks, street lights, shops with plate-glass windows and signs in English. Twenty-five foreign airlines are headquartered on Durbar Marg and nearby Kanti Path (King's Way), as well as many of Kathmandu's one hundred travel and trekking agencies and several luxury hotels. When a member of the royal family chooses to go out, blue-uniformed policemen line the streets to stop all traffic.

King Birendra, the world's only Hindu monarch, is a man of as much paradox as the kingdom he rules. He is a contemporary man, the product of Eton and Harvard, and one of the world's wealthiest men. He is considered the reincarnation of the Hindu god Vishnu, yet he must bow each year to a virgin girl goddess, the Royal Kumari, to ask permission to continue his reign. As the king's sleek black Mercedes whizzes from the palace, there is but a glimpse of a mustached man in dark glasses. The best way to get a closer look is to enter any shop or hotel, where, inevitably, the faces of king and queen peer from framed photographs, a solemnly gazing couple in their early forties. The king's head is covered by a flat red-orange-and-white-printed topi, the traditional Nepali hat; the queen wears a bouffant hairdo, circa 1965.

The activities of the royal family are reported in excruciating detail by Nepal's major daily newspaper, *The Rising Nepal*, with reportage on a par with a small-town weekly. A typical front-page item: "His Royal Highness the Crown

Prince has returned to the United Kingdom for his studies after spending a few weeks' vacation . . ." and no issue is complete without King Birendra's quote of the day. Example: "All of us should now concentrate our energies on the task of national construction and economic development, steering clear of useless political polemics."

Just a few blocks west of the palace is a very different scene, Thamel, a trippie paradise of two-dollar lodges and dollar-a-meal restaurants, the getting-off place for treks to the Himalaya or expeditions to the jungles of the Terai. It is another separate reality, a vast open-air boutique, a harmonious intersection of mountains and jungle, Tibet, Nepal, India, and the world.

The streets swarm with pedestrians in bright nylon gear, seemingly an international convention of backpackers, speaking English in every conceivable accent and every tongue of Europe and Asia. Shops strung with sleeping bags and down jackets are a reminder of the proximity of the Himalaya. An elephant with "Happy Birthday" written across its side in red vermilion powder represents the nearby jungle of the Terai. Indian men in loincloths vend bananas and oranges from bicycles. Tibetans sell old masks, carpets, strands of turquoise, prayer wheels, and multicolored striped sweaters. Nepali tailors stitch bright cottons into instant copies of Western skirts, shirts, and trousers. Used paperback bookstores offer English-language selections ranging from Charles Dickens to Judith Krantz.

Thamel's restaurants are a smorgasbord of everything Western, in infinite variety, if not certain quality. One can choose from apple strudel at the Old Vienna Inn, pizza at Marco Polo, cappuccino at La Dolce Vita, momos at Tibet's Kitchen, buffalo steak at KC's, draft beer at Spam's Spot Pub, quiche at La Bistro, borscht at Red Square, apple pie at Helena's, or spring rolls at China Town. There are croissants, baguettes, and bagels. The one cuisine absent from the repertoire is Nepal's traditional dal bhat—lentils, rice, and vegetables.

Ragamuffin boys stand at street corners, supplicants chanting a mantra of frenzied hustle. "Caaaar-pet, caaaar-pet . . ." lowers to a soft, "Change money? We give more than bank," to a barely audible "Hash?" with a surreptitious opening of the palm to reveal what looks like a black ball of mud. There are plenty of takers for all three commodities. A Tibetan carpet triples in value back home; the black-market dollar exchange rate is 20 percent above the bank rate; and twenty dollars buys an ounce of hash.

Not far from Thamel, six streets converge at Asan Tol, the major stop on the Tibet-Kathmandu-India trading route. Thamel may be a crossroads of the world, but here is the crossroads of countless smaller worlds, the stage where the many ethnic groups of the Himalaya converge to play out an eternal drama of barter. No attempt at a modern shopping center has displaced Asan and its environs as the major marketplace of the valley. Newari vendors sit barefoot, cross-legged on straw mats, voices rising and falling to haggle over vegetables, fruits, grains, and spices, weighed out on hand scales. Every space is covered with produce, including the steps of the Annapurna and Ganesh temples. Merchandise

Bodhanath stupa surrounded by monasteries and a circle of souvenir shops, formerly owned and run by Newari silversmiths and goldsmiths who traded with Tibet. Bodhanath continues to be a trading and pilgrimage center for Tibetans who come to the valley in the winter months.

Legend says the stupa was built by Kangma, a girl of supernatural birth, to honor Buddha Amitabha. The dome is set on a platform in the shape of a mandala and supports a tappered gilded pinnacle. Prayer flags, offered by pilgrims, stretch the length of the stupa, and the white painted dome has yellow paint markings signifying petals of the lotus.

Hanuman Dhoka Durbar was once the residence of the Malla kings and early Shah dynasty. The palace name honors the guardian monkey god, Hanuman, a great patron of the Mallas; they claimed descent from Ram Chandra, whose devotion to Hanuman was legendary. Some of the finest woodcarving in the Kathmandu Valley is visible inside the palace. Close by stands the grand Taleju temple, built in 1564 by Mahendra Malla. The worship of the Taleju goddess arrived with refugees from the south; she became the guardian deity of the Malla kings.

spills from the doorways of roadside shops. There is order within the chaos, since many items have occupied the same place for centuries. But old is mingled with new. Traditional pots of brass and copper are sold by the kilo alongside the stainless steel and aluminum cookware that is beginning to replace them. There are traditional pottery water pots, but also plastic jugs.

The narrow streets resound with jingling rickshaw bells, the beep of motorcycle horns, and the deeper note of car horns. People jam the narrow streets. Bells ring from the temples, and flute music wafts from the distance. Flocks of pigeons descend, wings rustling, to fight for spilled grain. Sacred cows wander at random, munching on scraps of refuse. Not far away, Seto Machhendranath, revered god of the valley, is worshiped by Buddhists as well as Hindus.

The schooled ear can discern intonations of Nepali, Newari, Tamangi, Tibetan, Hindi, and countless other languages; the knowing eye can identify the diversity of ethnic groups. The men in traditional tie-wrapped jackets and baggy pants, shoulders hoisting wooden poles hung with basketsful of giant radishes, are Newari Jyapu farmers. The women whose noses and ears are heavy with gold ornament are Tamangi, of Tibeto-Burmese stock. There are Nepali men in topis—Nepal's national headgear—Tibetan women in thick woolens, and turbaned Indian Sikhs.

While Asan Tol perpetuates the past, The Supermarket, a short walk away on the aptly named New Road, pushes toward the present. It is the Nepali answer to a Western shopping center, complete with Kathmandu's first and only public escalator. The escalator is so popular a guard on each floor is required to hold back the crowds who jam the entrance. The Supermarket and the surrounding shops of New Road represent Kathmandu's bid for twentieth-century-style consumerism. But the price tags on the shiny new refrigerators, washing machines, VCRs, and televisions—all from Hong Kong—include hefty import duties that put them out of the reach of all but the very rich. Nevertheless, business is brisk, with members of Nepal's newly emerging middle class flocking in to buy the more affordable items, such as small appliances, cassette tapes, running shoes, and cosmetics. Video cassette rentals are a booming business, with selections ranging from *Gone With the Wind* to *Rambo.*

If consumerism is the god of New Road, the valley's other gods are not far away—at nearby Durbar Square, a ten-acre complex of temples and palaces, where benign gods reign peacefully, where thirsty gods demand blood sacrifice, where a living goddess still watches the world from a lonely temple window.

Here are temples that manifest the grandeur of the past, an eloquent backdrop to the more tawdry present. Three towers of the Durbar symbolize ancient kingdoms of the valley, Bhaktapur, Lalitpur, and Kirtipur. Temples to the gods Shiva and Narayan, goddesses Parvati and Taleju rise in pyramiding steps to tiered pagoda roofs, reaching upward, like the snow peaks on the northern horizon. The pagoda, an architectural reflection of the Himalayan peak, originated in the temples of the Kathmandu Valley in the seventh century and later spread across China and Japan.

Each god's personality reflects an aspect of the human experience. There are the angry demon Bhairav and his bloodthirsty wife, Durga; the wise elephant, Ganesh; the monkey leader, Hanuman; the mystical goddess, Taleju; and hundreds of other small and large gods of the Hindu pantheon.

At the western edge of Durbar Square, three tiers of pagoda roof rise fifty feet upward above a long veranda, a structure known as Kasthamandap, where vendors of vegetables sit with their radishes and onions, greens and tomatoes. What appears to be a simple vegetable market is actually the oldest surviving timber structure in the valley, the building that named the valley and the city. While exotic to the Western ear, *Kathmandu* is nothing but prosaic when the words of its origin are translated: "Wooden House."

Historically, it is known that the Kasthamandap was a rest house for holy men on their long treks across the trade route between Tibet and India. It was built in the eleventh century on an ancient river site. In a factual world, one would assume that its supporting timbers were cut from some great forest. But no history of the Kathmandu Valley begins or ends in historical fact. Factual history is available only in fragments, from ancient inscriptions on stone slabs, fountains, buildings, and monuments, and from a few written accounts left by early travelers.

But myth and legend are abundant, available in many versions, told and retold through the generations by a people who put great value on the written word. Myth and legend, products of the universal quest for the truths of life, are unique and original in Kathmandu because of the isolation of the valley; they are exotic and mysterious to Western ears because the philosophies that have shaped them are not our own.

Thus the history of Kasthamandap begins in the time when the valley was the entire universe, where great gods of Hindu and Buddhist mythology roamed, challenging omniscient powers one against the other, warring, loving, performing heroic deeds, and conferring gifts of power that turned mortal men to kings. Kasthamandap's timbers belong to these epic dramas of prehistory, a celestial tree given by the gods, with instructions to build the city now called Kathmandu. Such happenings were, and are, the nature of the valley.

LAND

OF THE GODS

No aspect of life in Kathmandu—political, historical, or cultural—can be separated from the legends of gods that dominated the past and still inspire much of the drama of daily life.

Gods are everywhere, in the water, the sky, plants, rocks, animals, and living people. Some are indigenous to the valley, while others were imported from Hindu epics such as the Ramayana and the Mahabharata. There are three million deities in Hindu texts—three times as many gods as residents of the Kathmandu Valley. A single god can take thousands of forms. Gods can switch to each others' forms and take on opposing qualities and duties, manifesting all the complexities of human nature. Their multiple hands and heads connote superhuman power; they take consorts and possess vehicles of transportation. They can be snakes, cows, crows, or bees. They can be mortal beings, virgin girls or kings. They convey every form of human emotion. There are scowling, fighting, murdering gods; wise gods, laughing gods, sensual gods. Gods of mercy cause the sun to shine, the wind to blow, the rivers to flow. Gods of wrath bring violent storms, earthquakes, and famine.

The gods are loved. The gods are feared. Their worship never seems to cease, in constant rituals and festivals in the home and on public streets. One works to keep in favor with the gods, smearing the forehead with vermilion powder and dabs of rice, making constant puja offerings. Hungry gods must be fed with tasty morsels of rice, fruit, and sweets. Thirsty gods demand water, milk, and the flowing blood of sacrifice.

The domination of the gods is intensified by the simultaneous practice of Buddhism and Hinduism in worship patterns unique to Nepal. In India, Hinduism dates to 1700 B.C., Buddhism to 500 B.C. The valley's Buddhists and Hindus

---

Swayambhu floating above a sea of clouds. It is believed that when the valley's lake drained, the Self-Existent One radiated as a flame from a lotus blossom atop this hill.

27

Gilded Garuda, or bird man, the traditional steed of Vishnu.

Portraying Lord Krishna in the fighting "musthi mudra" position inside Patan's Mul Chowk, built by Siddhinarasingha in 1660 and dedicated to the mother-earth goddess Durga. On the northeast corner stands the Taleju temple.

Samyak festival in Patan, with a line of Dipan-kara Buddhas receiving offerings of food from Newari devotees.

The all-seeing eyes of the supreme Buddha stare out in each cardinal direction from the gilded spire of the Swayambhu stupa. The red spiral "question mark" denotes dharma—virtue—a path to self-awareness.

Despite the chilly winter morning, Managi women prostrate themselves before stone Buddha statues at the base of Swayambhu hill.

often share the same gods, philosophies, mythologies, and places of worship. Even certain conflicting philosophies, such as the Hindu belief in a caste system, coexist in harmony.

Hindu and Buddhist legends often overlap and intertwine with each other and with animistic legends of the Nagas, the valley's prehistoric snake gods. For the earliest legends of Kathmandu begin in prehistory, the era that archaeologists call the Pleistocene Period, a million years ago. The valley was Naga-vala, "Abode of the Snake Gods," a vast turquoise lake writhing with snakes and reptilian monsters. At the center of the lake was a mystical lotus, "Swayambhu," a primordial buddha that deified the waters and brought gods and goddesses, buddhas and bodhisattvas to worship from the shores.

The lotus was round as a chariot wheel, with ten thousand petals of gold, pollen of rubies and diamonds, stamens of gold, and pistils of lapis lazuli. From its center emanated the mystical blue light of a flame purer and brighter than the sun. Its renown drew one of the supernatural princes of Buddhism, the Bodhisattva Manjushri, from northern China.

When Manjushri saw the lotus he lifted his mighty sword of wisdom and sliced the valley wall with a powerful blow. The waters ebbed away, leaving a fertile valley laced with rivers. The lotus glowed brighter still, and from beneath it, a hill emerged, Devbhumi, "Home of the Gods." There Manjushri built a shrine, Swayambhunath (the suffix *nath* means "place"), which has been held sacred through the ages.

Close to the Swayambhu stupa there is an important shrine, the Harati Ajima, a two-tiered, Hindu-influenced temple harboring an image of Bhagbati. According to local belief, this deity protects children from disease, especially smallpox; it is common to see parents here with children petitioning a blessing. The woman pictured here is believed to be a reincarnation of Ajima and is often solicited by parents for counsel and blessing.

OPPOSITE

Situated at the base of Swayambhu stupa rests a huge gilded vajra, called the thunderbolt or diamond sceptor, which is said to represent the power of Buddha's omnipresent knowledge. It is a symbol of male energy and suggests the immutable, awakened, empty self and the skillful exercise of wisdom.

On the full-moon day of Lord Buddha's birth, a picture of the Dalai Lama is carried around the Swayambhu stupa by Buddhist monks.

The curious shape of Chobar Gorge, a unique geological formation at the edge of the Bagmati River in the south of the valley, provides visible evidence of the legend. The hillside appears sliced, and below, nestled in a gorge, bodies are cremated on a temple ghat so that the ashes can be strewn into a river that eventually converges with the holy Ganges of India.

The smoke of cremation rises in thin wisps and mingles, a hundred yards beyond, with the heavy, puffing smoke of the Chobar Cement Plant. A booming blast of dynamite showers limestone toward the river, a jarring reminder of the present.

A mile north of Chobar Gorge, it is easy to return to the spell of the past. There stands Swayambhunath, rising high on a hill overlooking the center of Kathmandu. Whatever the truth of the legends of origin, the "self-born" stupa

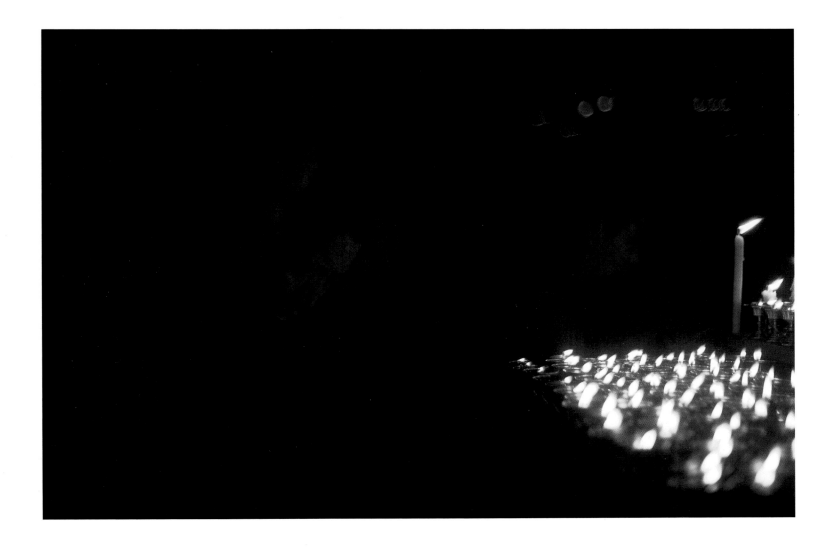

has existed at least twenty centuries. It rises atop a forested hill, staring with four sets of lotus eyes from beneath a conical roof rising gold into the sky. Bands of rhesus monkeys frolic on the long staircase leading up to the stupa's base, where 211 prayer wheels spin clockwise in continual supplication to the heavens. An eternal procession of believers, both Buddhist and Hindu, circumambulate the building, prostrating themselves along their circular path, chanting the Buddhist mantra, *om mani padme hum*, "Hail to the Jewel in the Lotus."

If Swayambhunath is the valley's premier Buddhist monument, its Hindu peer is Pashupatinath, with the site dating to 500 B.C. and temple buildings to A.D. 200, on the Bagmati River five miles northwest of Kathmandu's center. Swayambhunath is like a head and shoulders emerging from a hilltop, contemplative, regal, wise. Pashupatinath is a heart, a complex mass of temples, a gath-

To acquire merit, Managi women prostrate themselves around the circular road at the base of Swayambhu.

ering place of throbbing streams of people beside the waters of the holy Bagmati River beside it. Pashupatinath houses the sacred image of the Hindu god Shiva, a phallic lingam carved with faces and endowed with supernatural powers.

As one of the three gods of the Hindu triad, Shiva rules the world alongside Brahma and Vishnu. Brahma, the creator, made heaven and earth. Vishnu, the preserver, saves the earth under various incarnations, including Rama, hero of the Ramayana epic, Krishna, hero of the Mahabharata epic, and Narayan, the embodiment of universal love and humanity. Shiva, the destroyer, who takes at least sixty-four diverse forms using 1,008 different names, is the god who most dominates the imagination of the people of the Kathmandu Valley. In the days of the gods upon earth, Shiva tired of the cloying admiration of lesser deities and changed to a gazelle for an anonymous frolic in the forest. The gods angrily seized

Temple grounds of Pashupatinath, holiest Hindu shrine in Nepal and a major cremation site. Immersing the feet of a dying person in the Bagmati River releases the soul; after death, the body is cremated on a riverside ghat. The two-tiered gilded temple, dedicated to Shiva (as Pashupati, Lord of the animals), dates from 1696.

A Hindu ascetic, or sadhu, has renounced his caste ties and embraced a life dedicated to Shiva.

OPPOSITE, LEFT

Shiva lingams sit inside yonis, symbolizing the unity between male and female energies. The lingam is Shiva in his universal form and is a bestower of fertility.

OPPOSITE, TOP RIGHT

A sadhu rests by Shiva's vehicle, Nandi the bull, in the peaceful area of Gujewari.

OPPOSITE, BOTTOM RIGHT

In Sanskrit literature, Shiva is exalted under 1,008 names and worshiped in countless manifestations, each known for certain powers. It is Shiva as the brooding, long-haired ascetic that sadhus emulate by renouncing the world and freeing themselves from the bondage of sensual passion. This sadhu wears a wooden chastity belt.

him by a horn, which broke off to become a lingam, Shiva's phallic form. Dense vegetation and mud buried the lingam in the forest until it was discovered in the dramatic event that gave the valley its earliest name.

A sacred cow wandered in the forest to a place at which—enigmatically—milk began to gush unbidden from her teats. Astounded cow herders dug into the mud of that place until the lingam rose up in the form of a terrible flame. Many deities came to worship at this place, including the goddess Yoghini, who asked Ne, a sultan hermit, to cover the flame to protect it. The name *Ne* and the word *pal*—"protection"—became "Nepal," the original name of the Kathmandu Valley, which later came to designate the entire country.

The temple built on this sacred site is Pashupatinath, a name connoting Shiva's identity as the gentle shepherd of the souls of men. (But the omniscient Shiva is also manifest as a dope-smoking ascetic, a frenzied dancer, a raging demon, and the fertile "Lord of Coition.") It is Shiva, in the form of Pashupati, of all the thousands of gods of the valley, that most influences the day-to-day life of Nepal. Each morning at six A.M., Radio Nepal begins its daily program with a hymn to Pashupatinath. Kings are cremated at ghats of the Pashupatinath temple. Medieval kings built copies of the temple within their own vast temple/palace complexes, and Pashupatinath is emblazoned on the royal coat of arms.

Shiva's sculpted lingam is a ubiquitous icon of the valley, in sizes as small as a fist or as tall as a tree. It can be the simplest pile of molded sand or cow dung or an elaborate sculpture of stone. At Pashupatinath, lingams grow like shrubs from Kailash Hill and grow around one temple like engorged mushrooms, sixty-four of them springing upward from the yoni platforms that are symbolic wombs. Shiva lingams mark the graves of yogis—sadhus—buried, in the lotus position, in pits filled with salt. Sometimes the lingam takes a more literal phallic form. At a Pashupatinath temple housing a sculpture of Shiva's wrathful form, Bhairav, the figure's erect penis is united with the living flesh by women who furtively touch their private parts to the cold stone to gain fertility.

The cult of the Shiva lingam originates with a drunken orgy at the god's legendary paradise retreat near Mount Kailash in Tibet. A scornful, mocking delegation of Hindu gods witnessed the display of self-indulgence, and the mortified Shiva died, proclaiming that he would thenceforth take the form of the lingam: "The lingam is I, my double self. . . . All should worship and offer sacrifice to it as if to me."

The original Shiva lingam, probably the most revered icon in Nepal, is cloistered beneath the double-tiered gold pagoda of the main temple of Pashupatinath, behind silver doors. A sculpture of Shiva's bull, Nandi, kneels reverently before one door, a massive gilded icon ten feet long and five feet high, with diamond eyes, hoofs of solid silver, and horns and tail of solid gold.

Multitudes of Hindu worshipers circumambulate the temple, necks adorned with the ridged brown seeds of the rudraksha tree, symbolic of the powers of Shiva. Hindus dance, sing, and chant *om nama shivaya*, "I bow to Shiva," offering holy water, sweets, flowers, and sacred leaves. They reverently touch the bull's

testicles and enter the temple to pay homage to the lingam inside. It is three feet of black stone carved with five faces of Shiva. The smooth upper face is believed to be infused with the energy of sun, fire, and femininity. It is said to be so hot it will instantly dry water and has the power of turning base metal into gold. But only the high priest, an Indian-born Brahmin, is allowed to touch it. Each day, this priest conducts elaborate rituals in accordance with a strict schedule:

4 A.M.	Temple doors open.
9:30 A.M.	The god is undressed.
9:45 A.M. to 12:30 P.M.	The lingam is bathed in holy water from the Bagmati; priests sing hymns to Shiva.
1 to 1:30 P.M.	Priests dress the lingam in golden cloth, perfume it with incense, and let it gaze into the mirror.
1:30 P.M.	Temple doors close; the god is fed rice, pudding, sweets, fruit, vegetables, chutney, and water.
6:30 P.M.	Temple doors reopen.
7 to 8 P.M.	Water is offered from a conch shell, and the god worshiped with singing and prayers.

Gifts have made Pashupatinath wealthy; large parcels of real estate are held in the temple's name, including Tribhuvan International Airport, which the government leases through an annual payment. The diamond, gold, and silver bull, Nandi, was a gift of atonement from a prime minister who accidentally shot a cow in the Nepal Terai in 1939.

The Bagmati River, a shallow, murky tributary of the Ganges, flows by the temple of Pashupati. There the devout bathe, beneath the pale disk of the moon and in the glare of the sun, in the dawn of morning and the twilight of evening. Men, women, and children descend from the temple to wade in the river, bending with cupped hands to lift the holy water to their lips. Bands of rhesus monkeys swing down from the temple roof to frolic alongside the bathing worshipers. At its source high on the northwest rim of the valley, the Bagmati flows from a sculpted tiger mouth. It is a revered place, where it is said Shiva's tears once dripped to begin the river current that flows southward to the holy Ganges.

Bagmati's murky waters are believed to be purifying, endowing those who bathe there with certain spiritual benefits, including fulfillment of earthly desires and eventual salvation, freedom from the karmic cycle of birth and rebirth. Husbands and wives bathe together in the Bagmati in order to be married partners in the afterlife. Failure to bathe in the river, or committing the sacrilege of wear-

THIS PAGE AND OPPOSITE

Pagalinanda Agore Baba, sixty-six years old, performs asanas inside his den alongside the Pashupatinath cremation ghats. Agore Babas are known for demonstrating their transcendence of worldly pain by such extreme acts as eating the flesh of corpses, drinking their own urine, and lifting heavy stones suspended from their penises.

Hindu pilgrims from India descend the stone stairs at Pashupatinath to take a purifying dip in the holy Bagmati River.

Indian Hindu pilgrims washing along the banks of Pashupatinath.

Mirrored images of Hindu pilgrims drying cotton saris along the banks of the Bagmati River.

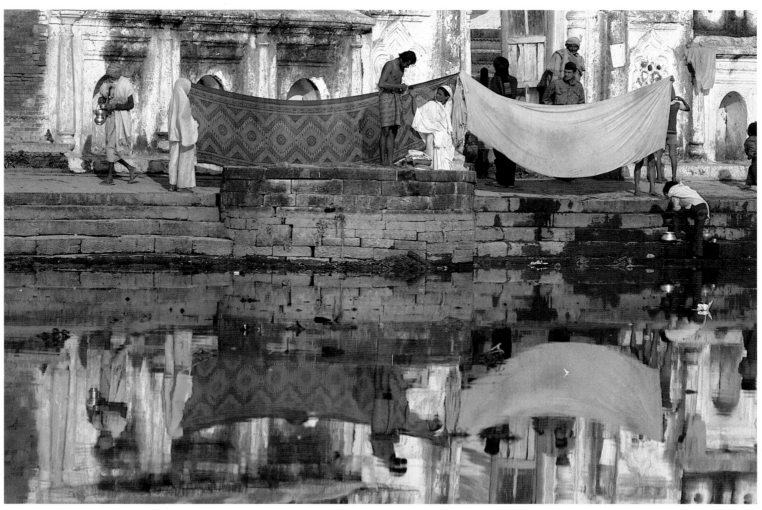

In a Hindu family, only a son can conduct the last rites—sraddha—the all-important ceremony that sends the soul on its journey. Riven by grief, the youngest son in this family must cremate his mother.

Brothers watch their mother's cremation.

ing shoes into it, brings punishment in the next life—rebirth as a miserable animal.

In the Hindu faith one lives by rituals and dies by rituals. There are ceremonies to name a baby and bestow its first solid food, ceremonies for the first haircut, and for all of life's subsequent phases. Death and cremation on the banks of the Bagmati is considered a most auspicious way to end one's days, particularly if it takes place at Pashupatinath. A continual drama, an assembly line of death unfolds at the foot of the temple, open to the observation of the most casual of tourists. Just up the river banks from the main temple stands a plain rectangular building, a house of death. Those inside have been proclaimed by an astrologer to be in the last hours of life. Down at the river's edge lies a special stone, at the

Ritual cremation along the banks of the Bagmati, Pashupatinath.

Cremation pyres burn along the banks of the sacred Bagmati, which carries ash back into the eternal cycle of life.

foot of the same temple steps where the devout bathe, monkeys splash, and naked boys dive. To this place the dying man is taken in his last moments and lies, feet submerged in the waters, while attendants lift a handful of water to his gasping mouth—the "last water." The Hindu believer dies content that his "good death" will enhance his position in the next life. Life is suffering; death is release.

The dead body is washed in the river, and within an hour it is bound in yellow cloth, the color of marigolds, and carried on a stretcher a few hundred feet farther along the river, where a half-dozen cremation platforms extend into the river, the scene of continual activity. At one, men lay logs in thigh-high layers, forming the shape of a single bed. At another, a sweeper unceremoniously rakes ashes into the river. At a third, a cluster of mourners, white-robed men with shaven heads, sit watching flames lapping at a charred human leg.

There is always a certain smell to the air here, the odor of wood smoke laced

with the powerful, acrid smell that emanates from the burning of human flesh. Tourists prowl a ledge above the cremation ghats. Camera shutters snap. Faces watch, some curious, intent; some tearful; others laughing nervously. Close-ups on death are not so available back home.

A new cremation begins. Sons arrive, dressed in white mourning robes that symbolize purity, their heads shaven (the gods don't like hair). Death is a community event. The wood has been purchased by a neighborhood association, the body carried by friends. The family's women stay home to mourn; only sons attend the cremation.

Only a son can conduct life's final rites of sraddha, the all-important ceremony that sends the soul on its journey, lighting a bit of camphor in the mouth of the corpse, daubing bits of rice and flowers onto the forehead, chanting, "Now you go to your god so you don't have to come to this life again and again." The eldest son conducts sraddha for his father; the youngest for his mother. The birth of a son is of utmost importance to every family; for without a son to perform the ceremony, the soul wanders eternity, a restless ghost.

After the ritual come the sounds of crackling fire. Temple bells gong, deep and mellow, and from a distant hill wafts the lonely melody of a flute and the thump of drums. The smoke rises and curls toward a nearby Shiva lingam, believed to carry the departed soul closer to salvation. Burning a human body is a long process, and it is hours before the pile of ashes is swept into the Bagmati.

The sluggish current carries them southward, through the maze of temples clustered around Pashupatinath, where stand temples to the gods Bhairav, Vishnu, and Rama, where lingams perch atop yonis, and nagas writhe on temple struts, where images of Ganesh, Garuda, Laxmi, Krishna, Saraswati, and Buddha keep congenial company.

The ashes drift through Chobar Gorge, flowing from the valley just as the first waters flowed through the sword cut of Manjushri, flowing on to the holy Ganges of India and back into the eternal cycle of life dominated by the gods.

The Manohara River, west of Changu Narayan, snakes its way through the Kathmandu Valley.

KINGDOMS PAST

Through the long drift of centuries, gods of the Kathmandu Valley bestowed the power of kings, while ordinary men accepted the judgment. Even now, the king of Nepal arrives at Durbar Square on a designated day each year to bow humbly before the child goddess of Kathmandu, the Royal Kumari, a virgin of perfection and self-possession worshiped as the reincarnation of the goddess Taleju. The Kumari bestows the king's powers with the application of a tikka, the "third eye" of Hinduism, placed at the center of his forehead.

The king, of course, possesses his own supernatural powers, as the reincarnation of the god Vishnu, preserver of the universe, who soars about the skies, keeping watch over earth, heaven, and hell. Such reincarnation is a distinction the king shares with Buddha, the ammonite fossils strewn in the Kali Gandaki riverbed northwest of the valley, and the fruit of the wood-apple tree. Divine kings ruled Nepal from the Kathmandu Valley for two thousand years, perpetuating systems of heredity and favor that concentrated wealth and power in the hands of a few.

Gods are credited with the creation of the first civilizations of the Kathmandu Valley. After the powerful Bodhisattva Manjushri sliced Chobar Gorge to create the Kathmandu Valley, he built towns as homes for his disciples. Manjushri laid out a city in the form of a sword on the fertile lands where the Bagmati

---

The greatest contributors to the cultural heritage of Nepal were from the Malla dynasty, founded in 1350 by Jayastithi-Malla. Their six-hundred-year reign ushered in many great artistic and architectural achievements. The valley was divided among the three sons of Yaksa Malla into Kantipur, Lalitpur, and Bhaktapur, today known as Kathmandu, Patan, and Bhaktapur. Disunity and competitiveness resulted from this division. The disunity was the main cause of the defeat of the Mallas at the hands of Prithivi Narayan Shah; the spirit of competition spurred the creation of spectacular temples and palaces. One of the greatest patrons of art and architecture in this sixth-century period was King Bhupatindra Malla (1696–1722) of Bhaktapur, shown here praying before the golden gate entrance to the Taleju temple.

River met the Vishnumati, the city that later became Kathmandu. And he created Lalitpur, today's Patan, on a nearby hillside, laid out as Buddha's "Wheel of Law," around a magnificent temple of golden gates and windows glistening with emeralds and precious stones.

The residents of these early cities were a people known as the Kiratis (ancestors of the Newars), who probably migrated to the valley from the eastern Himalaya in about 700 B.C., and were a dominant presence for about a thousand years. The Kirati civilization was heavily influenced by Buddhism, beginning at the time of Buddha's birth in southwestern Nepal, about 500 B.C. Though it is believed that Buddha never visited the Kathmandu Valley himself, his disciples traveled the trade route from India to Tibet, attracted by the legendary Swayambhu.

At Swayambhu and across the landscape they built stupas, domed places of worship that symbolize the enlightenment of the mind of Buddha. Four high grassy mounds still stand prominently on the landscape of Patan, a visible legacy of the Kirati era, probably built about 300 B.C. by the Indian emperor Ashoka, a Buddhist disciple.

The Ashoka stupas had been standing for six hundred years when the Licchavis invaded the valley from India in about A.D. 300, bringing their Hindu caste system, a social structure that dramatically changed Nepali civilization and still wields a profound influence. The caste system stratified downward from priests. Licchavis worshiped cows, practiced polygamy, and expected widows to immolate themselves upon the dead husband's funeral pyre. The Licchavis ruled five hundred years. By the end of this era, the religious practices they introduced had come to coexist harmoniously with the worship of primordial nagas and Buddhist stupas. Hindu temples went up alongside existing Buddhist stupas, and a new form of worship emerged, the cult of tantrism, which emphasized female sexual energy.

Artworks from the Licchavi period are preserved at the temple of Changu Narayan, including the oldest known inscription in the Kathmandu Valley, dated A.D. 467, on a pillar dedicated to the fifth-century Licchavi king, Manadeva I. Licchavi kings were the absolute monarchs of scores of petty kingdoms, adorning themselves with pearls, jade pendants, and gold earrings, and inhabiting opulent, gem-studded palaces. Their reign was first concentrated at Patan, but due to the intervention of the goddess Taleju, the kingdom of Bhaktapur, nine miles to the east, emerged as the central power of the valley.

Like most valley legends, the story of Bhaktapur has a fairy-tale quality. "Once upon a time"—sometime in prehistory—the god Indra meditated a thousand years on the god Shiva and received a mysterious reward, a "yantra," a mystic diagram endowed with the magical powers of Taleju. The shape may have represented shakti, the divine female power worshiped by tantrists, but no one is certain, for it was seen only by the eyes of kings.

The yantra was hidden for aeons, until Taleju informed the Licchavi king Nanya Dev of its whereabouts—in a golden box beneath a swarm of buzzing bees

Changu Narayan temple, dedicated to Vishnu. The temple, destroyed at the beginning of the eighteenth century, dates to the fifth century. Surrounding it are stone sculptures from the Licchavi period (A.D. 400–900), including the oldest Licchavi inscription in the valley, found on the victory pillar erected in A.D. 464 by King Manadeva I.

at a river bank. Alongside the yantra was a magic sword, which the king used to slay a monster serpent and thereby take possession of ancient wells filled with gold, silver, and precious stones: enough wealth to found a kingdom.

The yantra passed from king to king, endowing each with the powers of Taleju, until the Tirhutian king Hari Singh Dev brought it to the place that is now Bhaktapur, "city of devotees," and there built a temple to Taleju. Bhaktapur became the ruling kingdom of the valley and remained so until the eighteenth century.

During the Licchavi period, an ethnic group known as the Newars appeared, a people with cultural roots as diffuse as the entangled religions of the valley. Their origin, either from the south Indian plains or the northeast Himalaya, is still debated by scholars. Their language, Newari, was influenced by Indian Sanskrit, Tibeto-Burman, and the Kirati of the valley's first inhabitants. As talented artists, shrewd tradesmen, skilled craftsmen, and productive farmers, the Newars played a crucial role in the centuries that followed.

The Licchavi were succeeded by the Thakuri, who ruled from A.D. 900 to 1200 and who were in turn followed by the Mallas, Hindus of Rajput descent, who ruled until the fall of Bhaktapur to Prithivi Narayan Shah in 1769. Led by Malla kings, the Newars accomplished artistic and architectural achievements comparable to those of the European Renaissance. During this time, three independent rival kingdoms emerged—Kathmandu, Patan, and Bhaktapur—dense, walled cities built around vast Durbar Squares, complexes of palaces and temples housing both kings and gods. The highest castes lived at the centers of these cities, while the lowest inhabited the edges. Beyond the gates, farmers produced crops to support the feudal towns.

Malla kings lived flamboyantly, taking as many as three hundred wives, sending as many as thirty widows of a single king to deaths on flaming pyres, as dictated by the practice of sati. The Mallas not only conversed with gods, but declared themselves to *be* gods; in the fourteenth century, King Stithimalla de-

Representation of Vishnu, in the courtyard of the Changu Narayan temple.

RIGHT AND OPPOSITE

Representation of Vishnu (ca. A.D. 641) —asleep, reclining on a bed of snakes— in Budhanilkanta.

54

clared himself the reincarnation of Vishnu, a distinction claimed by all Nepali kings who followed.

The Mallas survived catastrophe, including famine and earthquakes that wiped out a third of the population, and Muslim invasions from India that destroyed much of Patan and Bhaktapur. A lucrative trade with Tibet financed ornate palaces and great temples at each of the Durbar Squares. The arts thrived in a wealth of forms, including bronze casting, metal work, stone carving, wood carving, thanka painting, and dance. The artistic renaissance spread to Tibet under the leadership of the gifted thirteenth-century Newari artist Aniko. The valley's original pagoda temple style spread north and east across Asia. And Tibet, by this time a Buddhist holy land, influenced the art and architecture of the Kathmandu Valley; the stupas of Swayambhu and Bodhnath were renovated in Tibetan style.

An Ex-Kumari of Kathmandu lives near the Durbar Square of Patan, in a couple of low-ceilinged rooms overlooking a narrow side street. She is a thin, barefoot old woman with graying hair, bony shoulders, and receding gums. Her eyes are recessed in deep sockets, her nails lined with dirt, and there are moles on her forehead and the bridge of her nose. Her long bones are aristocratic, yet the flesh is too skimpy and too slack, and when she stands she is no more than four feet high. Her only adornment is a key on a frayed string.

There are no chairs, so the ex-goddess sits on the windowsill of her small room, unfurnished but for a few grass mats scattered on the green-and-white linoleum. A single naked light bulb hangs from the low ceiling; fading blue paint chips from the walls. There is a broken radio, a tattered stool, and a clock with broken hands. Near the window, a foot-long tortoise stands still as a sculpture.

Her son, a young tailor dressed in white, translates as she recalls the days when King Tribhuvan and all the people of Kathmandu Valley paid homage. Then there were the later days, when she ceased to be a goddess.

Dil Kumari Sakya was proclaimed the Royal Kumari of Kathmandu when she was five, during the reign of King Tribhuvan, and was cloistered for seven years in the Kumari House at Durbar Square.

"I would look out the window and see other children play, and I also had the thought to want to go out and play. I would play like a butterfly. I would play stones and rock jacks. I would do puja, then bands would come and play music. I would watch them, and that was my day.

"When I was a goddess it was like that." She pauses to swat a housefly from her arm.

"When I left the Kumari I went to live with my mother and father, but I didn't want to stay. I just wanted to go back to the temple. Then they arranged my marriage to a Sakya.

"After I married it was difficult. I was accustomed to people worshiping me and bringing gifts. Once I became a wife I had to do the regular duties, carrying water, sweeping the floor, cooking rice. . . . I was a little bit lazy.

"My husband beat me and said, 'You're no good. You just stay here and shut up. You're

The rich legacy of the Malla period is still evident in the monumental architecture and art of the Durbar Squares of Patan, Bhaktapur, and Kathmandu, and in the work of countless Newar artists and artisans who carry on the traditions.

At each Durbar Square rises a temple to the goddess Taleju, "giver of existence," the goddess who took the form of the yantra, empowering Licchavi kings

The Taleju Mandir, built in 1564 by Mahendra Malla, is the most splendid and famous of the three Taleju mandirs built by the Mallas in the valley. The three-tiered roofs are of gilded copper edged with rows of wind bells.

to build their kingdoms. Malla kings continued to build great temples to Taleju and worshiped the goddess as their personal deity. Veneration of the goddess also took the form of virgin worship, the "cult of Kumari," which recurs in various legends of India and Nepal and has played a significant role in the history of the Kathmandu Valley.

In the eighteenth century, Jaya Praksha Malla, the Newar king of Kathmandu, drove Taleju to take virgin form; he gazed upon her with such lust in his heart that the offended goddess vanished, then reappeared in a dream, proclaiming, "O wretched King, your days are numbered and the fall of your dynasty is near. You shall no longer be blest with the sight of me. Select a girl child from a Newar caste, and I shall dwell in her body. Worship her as the Goddess Kumari, for to worship her is to worship me."

A child of the sakya, goldsmith, caste was selected to become the Kumari, a young girl whose physical beauty, courage, and emotional control were judged appropriate for a living goddess. She showed no fear in a dark chamber, where severed animal heads uttered strange cries, where masked demons leapt and shrieked. She was beautiful, her neck "like a conch shell," her eyelashes "like a cow's." She had never shed blood, neither through a cut nor through menstruation. And only she, as Taleju, could grant the king the right to rule.

Taleju's prophecy of the impending fall of the Malla dynasty came true. A calculated campaign to undermine the power of the Mallas began in 1742, when Prithivi Narayan Shah, the youthful prince of Gorkha, a kingdom to the northwest, first gazed from the edge of the valley at the walled kingdoms of Patan, Bhaktapur, and Kathmandu and proclaimed: "If I might be king of these three cities, why, let it be so."

Coveting rich valley farmlands as well as control of the lucrative Tibet trade, Shah waged a long, patient campaign, blockading the Tibetan and Indian trading route in order to weaken the Mallas economically. On the night of the September full moon, in 1768, military strategy and legend came together. Indra Jatra, one of the most lavish festivals of the valley, was in full swing at the Durbar Square of Kathmandu. The drunken bodies of the king's forces were strewn unconscious across the square, while that deified child, the Kumari, prepared to affirm, with a tikka on the forehead, King Jaya Praksha Malla's right to rule another year.

The Shahs marched into the undefended city, the Malla king fled, and Prithivi Narayan Shah bowed before the child goddess to receive Taleju's boon of power in the form of a blood-red tikka at the center of his forehead.

Within a year the Shahs also conquered Patan, Bhaktapur, and Kirtipur, thereby taking control of the entire valley. Bhaktapur's King Ranjit Malla, with the mystic Taleju yantra hidden beneath his cloak, was sent into exile in Benares.

The Shahs united the territory that is now the Kingdom of Nepal. Fearing a takeover from British-dominated India, they closed the country's borders in 1816, enforcing a very strict national policy of isolation that endured until the mid twentieth century.

Ex-Kumari of Kathmandu, Dil Kumari Sakya, holding her pet

worthless and lazy, and I'm going to leave you.'

"Each year I would go and see the new Kumari being pulled in the chariot, and my heart was sad."

As she speaks, the tortoise begins to plod with thick feet toward the window, eyes blinking. The ex-goddess picks it up and lovingly strokes the rough skin above its beak bill.

"My friends found me a second husband who did not beat me, and so I was happier. But he is dead now, and I am old. I don't know how to do much work, so my life is difficult."

Story finished, she changes to a white sari and poses for a few photographs, face brightening as the shutter snaps. "When I was a Kumari, many people came to take my picture, so I'm used to this."

Her son watches from a corner of the room. "What does it mean to have a mother who was a goddess?" he is asked.

He shrugs. "My mother was Kumari before my time, and it doesn't mean much to me."

57

The medieval flavor of Bhaktapur is apparent in the early morning fog, as residents, clad in thin cotton shawls, walk through Durbar Square, which is protected by life-size stone lion temple guardians. The present Durbar Square is a shadow of its former self, much of which was destroyed in a 1934 earthquake.

OPPOSITE

Bhaktapur, The Town of Devotees, glows at sunset, with Dorje Lakpa Himal rising 23,000 feet (center) behind one of the valley's architectural masterpieces, the Nayatapola temple in Taumadhi Square, built by Bhupatindra Malla in 1703. Bhaktapur is exclusively a Newar settlement.

The golden gate of Bhaktapur's Durbar Square—
the Sun Dhoka—erected by Ranjit Malla in
1753, is often compared to Ghiberti's famous
doors in the Baptistry in Florence, Italy. The
central figure of Taleju sits above the main doorway, with ten Hindu divinities set into the door
panels. The gilded Sanskrit inscription to the
right of the door praises the goddess Parvati,
while the inscription on the left, in the Newari
language, proclaims that King Ranjit Malla,
along with his queen, Jayalakmi, erected this
door to favor the goddess.

Perched beneath a massive stone lion guardian,
a Bhaktapur Newar absorbs the last rays of
sunshine.

A devotee discreetly salutes Narasimha, the angry man-lion incarnation of Vishnu, who is depicted here ripping open the belly of the demon Hiranyakasipu for terrorizing the mortals. Narasimha's anger was so great that it started to melt the earth. Shiva, in the form of the bird beast Saravha, descended to earth, snatched up Narasimha, and ascended to the heavens with him in order to quell his anger.

A Bhaktapur farmer stands in front of the Nyatapola temple, erected by Bhupatindra Malla in 1702 to favor Siddhi Laxshmi Devi, the goddess of wealth. Legend says that King Bhupatindra feared the goddess might grant his people more wealth than he possessed, so he and a tantric priest concealed the image for his worship alone.

At the base of the Nyatapola temple in Taumadi Square stands Jai Mal, the legendary wrestler of Bhaktapur from whom the Mallas took their name; he is reputed to have possessed the strength of ten men.

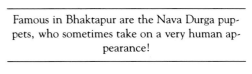

Famous in Bhaktapur are the Nava Durga puppets, who sometimes take on a very human appearance!

Whispering green wheat spreads across the intensely terraced landscape surrounding Bhaktapur town.

Bhaktapur women break apart clods of stubborn earth in preparation for planting wheat. Some farmers lease their fields to brick factory contractors, who take advantage of abundant blue clay found throughout the valley.

Newari Jyapus feeding pigeons.

Every available space is used at harvest time in Bhaktapur. Even alleyways serve as places for grain winnowing and drying.

The caste of potters in Bhaktapur is known as Kuma Prajapati; they live in the Taulachem and Talaco areas. Potting supplements their principal agricultural income and is carried out during lulls in farming activity. The Kathmandu Valley, once a lake bed, contains huge deposits of peat and phosphatic blue clay called kô. Due to a shortage of kilns, the clay pots are fired without an oven. The pots are stacked in circles of decreasing diameter smothered under wheat stalk, which is then packed with a thin covering of clay so that an impromptu "oven" is created.

Dattatraya, one of the finest and most renowned temples of Bhaktapur, is situated in Tachapal Tol and houses images of Shiva, Brahma, and Dattatraya, the Hindu trinity. The present structure was enlarged by Yaksha Malla in 1472 to function as a resthouse. The entrance is protected by the legendary wrestlers of Bhaktapur, Jai Mal, and Patta, who are flanked by the symbols of the deities inside. An image of Garuda is set on a pillar before the temple.

Legend describes Atraya as a sage whose wife, Anusurva, was revered by all for her beauty, chastity, and devotion to her husband. The reverence paid her angered the jealous wives of Brahma, Shiva, and Vishnu, who ordered their husbands to rape Anusurva. Disguised as sages, they approached her, begging for food and demanding that she serve it to them naked, lest the food be defiled. Anusurva realized they were gods and agreed to breastfeed them if they became six-month-old babies. They did so and, while suckling, were revolted by the thought of raping such a mother; they resolved instead to become her adopted sons. Datta (meaning adopted) was added to their names, customary in a patrimonial society, and they became wanderers and seekers after knowledge. Eventually, they settled in Tachapal Tol, where they constructed the Dattatraya temple. The entire square subsequently became a center of learning.

From the fourteenth century until their over-throw by Prithivi Narayan Shah in 1768, the Mallas created most of the artistic and architectural heritage evident throughout the valley today. The sun sets behind Bhaktapur's Durbar Square, silhouetting the impressive sikhara (an architectural style that originated in India) temple of Basala and the statue of Bhupatindra Malla raised on a pillar kneeling opposite the golden gate entrance to the Taleju temple.

A Newari carpenter carves graceful floral designs with a jigsaw. Much of the traditional woodcarving and design might have vanished without the recent conservation and restoration projects under way throughout the valley, sponsored by UNESCO and the Federal Republic of Germany.

When Lord Buddha returned to his birthplace in Lumbini, southwest Nepal, many modest women were eager to set eyes on the man. They ventured out on tree branches to shake scented petals to create a beautiful pathway for him. One woman fell from the tree, landing at Buddha's feet. He was so touched by this evidence of devotion that he proclaimed, *Let me be surrounded by these women.* Traditionally, especially in the Buddhist viharas (living and worshiping areas) inside Patan, wooden temple struts depict the ladies shaking branches as they face images of Buddha.

Wooden temple struts depicting the Asta Matrikas, mother-earth goddesses, together with
metal wind bells, line the Degu Talle temple
above Patan's Mul Chowk in Durbar Square.

Patan's theatrical performances traditionally were presented in the exquisitely constructed Mul Chowk, which features wooden struts carved with images of the Asta Matrikas and Asta Bhairabs. Natyeswari, goddess of theater, and the elephant god, Ganesh, grace the courtyard.

Ganesh sitting with his wife, Siddhi.

One of the Asta Matrikas slaying a demon.

The figure of Bagalamukhi, personification of one of the ten transcendental knowledges.

Stone carvings from Patan's Tusa Hiti, or royal worshiping bath of Sundari Chowk.

Shiva's manifestation as Nataraja, Lord of Dance, performs the Tandava dance during the time of destruction. In anger, a flame from his third eye destroys Kamadeva, the goddess of love, and turns her into ash. Mounted on Nandi the bull and flanked by musicians playing drums and cymbals, he also dances in pleasure. A masterpiece of medieval sculpture.

Mahila Shakya Silpakar, fifty-five years old, holding a mudra posture (ritual hand gesture) similar to that of the god Manjushri, who raises the sword of wisdom. Commissions by a few Newari and Tibetan Buddhists keep this ancient craft barely alive. In a melancholy voice, shaking his head, Mahila says, "In the old days these stone gods would speak to us, guiding our chisels along, but now we've broken too many rules, and there's only silence."

OVERLEAF

Sundari Chowk, in Patan's Durbar Square, was once the family residence of the Malla king Siddhinarasingha. Tusa Hiti, the extraordinary worshiping bath, is in the center of the square. The octagonal form of this tank accommodates the eight Nagas, rain goddesses. Lining the interior of the bath are many stone deities, including the Asta Matrikas (mother-earth goddesses), Asta Bhairabs, and the Asta Nagas. The gilded water spout shows Lord Vishnu and his wife, Laxmi, seated on their mount, the flying Garuda. Below the spout are aquatic animals, the fish, turtle, and crocodile, all representing the water, which falls from a conch shell. At the entrance to the bath is a stone slab where the king would sit, making offerings to all his favorite gods.

Stone sculpture of Uma Mahesvara, Sundhara, Patan.

In Bincha Bahal, Patan, a few families still carve
ivory. The life of Buddha is being carved into
this three-foot tusk, which will earn $3,500.00
for the carving family.

Newari men of Patan chisel detail into rough lost-wax castings. According to the casters, inflated prices for coal and beeswax hamper their craft.

OPPOSITE

A bronze statue of Ganesh with wife Siddhi
adorns the Bhimsen temple in Patan.

Newari women are employed to file smooth the
cast bronze images.

84

Splendid interlocking doorway design at Uku Bahal, one of Patan's most famous Buddhist monasteries. A shrine-keeper sits with the Dipankara Buddha image.

Kaji Ratna Shakya and his mother in front of
their store in Patan.

Inside Patan's Mul Chowk, Newari boys hold the alapadma mudra posture while performing the traditional dhime dance to the accompanying dhime drum. Drummer Siddhi Lal Maharjan is the only man left in the valley who knows the dance routine exactly.

Now used as government office space and backdrop for ceremonial occasions, the Hanuman Dhoka Palace of Kathmandu was once the private residence and official ceremonial grounds for the Malla kings and Shah dynasty. The temple structures were named after the ancient kingdoms, Lalitpur, Kirtipur, and Bhaktapur. On the northwest corner stands the five-tiered tower of the Panch Mukhi Hanuman, the five-faced monkey.

Southern face of the Hanuman Dhoka Palace,
with Nepalese merchants hawking souvenirs.

The Narayan temple

The Shah dynasty ended in 1846—less than a century after it began—in a bloody midnight massacre in a courtyard of Kathmandu's Durbar Square that eliminated the hundred most powerful men in Kathmandu. Thus began the Rana dynasty, a curious new century in the history of the Kathmandu Valley. Shah kings were stripped of power, but still worshiped as incarnations of Vishnu. The mastermind of the bloodbath, Jung Bahadur Kunwar Rana, declared himself prime minister and "maharaja," the first of the new dynasty.

He began his reign with an unprecedented voyage to Europe, taking along his seven brothers and enough cooks to observe the rigid eating and drinking restrictions of the Hindu caste sytem. For the first time in the history of Nepal, its royalty trod on Western soil, in London, Edinburgh, and Paris—with interesting results. The handsome maharaja cut a memorably exotic figure at the court of Queen Victoria, dressed in velvet robes trimmed in lace and studded with rubies, emeralds, diamonds, and pearls, topped by a plumed white silk cap glittering with diamonds and dangling with emeralds. The traveling Rana royalty found the palaces of Europe so impressive they began to replicate them, not an easy feat in an isolated mountain country still unconnected to the outside world by anything more than a walking trail.

In the rural fields of the valley, to which the rigid living codes of the past had exiled outcastes, the Ranas walled off vast estates and built colossal caricatures of the neoclassical palaces of Europe; they built the Red Palace, the White Palace, the Lion Palace, and many others. Armies of porters heaved furnishings up the mountain trails: crystal chandeliers, mirrors, window glass, marble tables and tiles, brocade chairs, iron lampposts, wrought-iron ornaments, and much more. The most magnificent palace was Singha Durbar, the Lion Palace, built in 1904 for Maharaja Chandra Shumsher Rana, sited on grounds half the size of the old walled city of Kathmandu and sumptuously fitted with imported European exotica.

Nor did the imitation of Europe stop with architecture. Inside the palaces, the Rana nobility and their many wives posed for formal photographs, dressed like parodies of Queen Victoria's court, as if they were revelers at some marathon costume ball. The trappings of male finery included plumed helmets, heavy epaulettes, long swords, tassels, braid, knee-high boots, gleaming escutcheons, white gloves, white trousers. The women became blimps in massive gathered skirts, bustles, and crinolines. Their hair was arranged in ringlets, framing heavily made-up faces topped with round, flat hats.

Into the twentieth century, the Ranas imported the latest inventions into the high walls of their palace compounds. They studied English, watched motion pictures, lit their palaces with electric bulbs, and even brought motor cars up the mountain trails on the backs of porters.

But extravagance was confined to the palace compounds. The Rana oligarchy administered Nepal like a private estate, leaving most of the people of the Kathmandu Valley more impoverished than ever, isolated from both the outer world and their own rulers. The Ranas enforced the rigid discrimination of the

Hindu caste system with the oppressive Mulki Ain of 1854, a law that assigned every section of the population of Nepal a place in the caste hierarchy. They did, however, abolish other savage customs, including human sacrifice, slavery, and sati—the self-immolation of widows.

The beginning of the end of the Rana regime came on January 15, 1934, a day as significant to twentieth-century Nepal as the stock market crash of 1929 is to the United States. It was the day the earth shook.

At 2:24 P.M. there were staccato noises and rumblings. The sky went dark, and for three minutes the Kathmandu Valley heaved like a ship in a tempest, cracking and splitting into wide crevasses. Bursts of earth and jets of hot water spewed into the air. Trees bent and were uprooted; roads crumbled. Inside the Rana palaces, mirrors and crystal chandeliers crashed, and electric bulbs burst in their sockets. Most of the White Palace crumbled to the earth. At the Durbar Squares, ancient palaces and temples cracked and leaned; many fell. Across the valley, the heaving earth leveled thousands of houses, tossing screaming men, women, and children into the air.

When the earthquake ended, thousands were crying out in pain and prayer, begging Varah, the earthquake god, to wake up from the terrible nightmare that caused the heaving of the earth. The death toll in the Kathmandu Valley was 4,296; three times that number were killed in the surrounding area.

The heaviest damage in the valley was in the Durbar Square of Bhaktapur. The rubble of temples and palaces was heaped around the sculpted boar image of Varah. The many pujas to the deity had failed to protect the valley; many, quite literally, had their faith in the power of the gods shaken. Varah was banished to a place of dishonor near the cremation ghats, and the long process of rebuilding began.

Within two months after the earthquake, another kind of upheaval began. An idealistic political movement formed around an alliance of three dissatisfied groups inspired by the independence movement of India. The ousted Shah monarchs were still endowed with the power of the gods, but not the power of men. They were restless. Also, Nepalese men had fought alongside the British in famed Gurkha regiments during both world wars; they returned home with new ideas from the outer world. Finally, the prolific reproduction rates among the polygamous Ranas created too many offspring to share the benefits of privilege peacefully. Juddha Shumsher Rana, maharaja at the time of the earthquake, had 130 wives. An "ABC" system was developed to rank Rana children according to the status of their mothers (primary wife, secondary wife, or concubine). Most were left disinherited and dissatisfied. In November 1950 the Shah king Tribhuvan launched a revolution based on the coalition of these three groups. On February 18, 1951, Tribhuvan took power, promising a new democratic government and an end to the long centuries of political isolation.

The white stucco Singha Durbar, the Lion Palace, built in 1904 for Maharaja Chandra Shumsher Rana. The waterscape approach was modeled after Versailles.

Maharaja Jung Bahadur Rana, the mastermind behind the Kot massacre, took control of the country in 1846, thus beginning the Rana Era during which the Shah monarchs were kept under house arrest or in exile in India. Returning from a trip to England, Jung Bahadur initiated the wearing of European attire at court and the building of white stucco European palaces.

Maharaja Chandra Shumsher came to power in 1901. He had Singha Durbar built, Kathmandu's largest palace and now the office of the Central Secretariat. Although Chandra criticized the British for educating the Indians, which he thought might create opponents to the Raj, he was responsible for setting up Trichandra College in Kathmandu. During his twenty-eight-year reign he abolished slavery and sati (self-immolation of widows) in Nepal as well as invited British engineers into the valley to build the first electric generating plants for Kathmandu and suspension bridges in the hill region. During Chandra's reign, foreign relations with the British were of great import. The British feared the expansion of Tsarist Russia into Tibet, which prompted Lord Curzon, viceroy in India, to send Captain Younghusband as leader of an expedition to sway the Tibetans to accept commercial and political relations with British-ruled India instead of with the Tsar. Chandra offered the assistance of Nepalese representatives in Tibet's capital, Lhasa, as arbiters between the British and the Tibetans. One result of this liaison was the inauguration of a trade route between India and Tibet via Sikkim. Unfortunately for Chandra and the Nepalese, the new route shifted commercial interest away from the old Kathmandu route. It is widely believed that Chandra was doing everything possible to keep the British away from Nepal, and he knew that if Tsarist Russia established itself in Tibet, the British would amass a border force along the Himalayas. Like Jung Bahadur Rana, Chandra stepped up recruitment of Gurkha soldiers to join the Indian army to help the British put down any uprising. He also sent Gurkhas to fight alongside the Allies in World War I. These actions prompted a treaty between Great Britain and Nepal, signed in 1923, which recognized Nepal's complete independence.

Maharaja Juddha Shumsher (1932–45) seated at Singha Durbar surrounded by his generals and wearing the insignia of the British GCV (Grand Master of the Bath). In 1934, Nepal was hit by a major earthquake, killing thousands and destroying many buildings. In the reconstruction phase, Juddha named what is now called New Road, the main commercial artery of Kathmandu, after himself, Juddha Sadak (street). After the earthquake, the family was caught in tremendous political upheaval. Too many illegitimate sons had been born to the Shumsher brothers, all of whom wanted to be on the "Roll of Succession" to the premiership. Risking assassination, Juddha purged the "B" and "C" class Ranas—those born to second wives and concubines—and banished them to the hill districts as governors. As Maharaja Chandra had done before him, Juddha pledged Gurkha soldiers to the British at the outbreak of war in 1939.

Prithivi Narayan Shah's daughter, Princess Tara Rajya Laxmi Rana, wife of General Krishna Shumsher, the son of Maharaja Chandra Shumsher.

Daughter of Prithivi Narayan Shah and wife of Sur Shumsher.

Wife of General Mrigendra Shumsher, the son of Babar Shumsher, who was Maharaja Chandra's second son.

Brahma Sumsher's wife, and the
daughter-in-law of Babar Shumsher.

105

His Majesty the late King Tribhuvan as a young boy. He would come to power in 1951, promising a new democratic government and an end to long centuries of political isolation.

Babar Shumsher's family, with sons Brahma and Mrigindra, both having graduated from the university at Patna, India.

Hunting tigers in Nepal's southern jungle. Left to right: King Mahendra and King Tribhuvan, along with Maharaja Juddha's youngest son, General Narayan Shumsher.

General Narayan Shumsher's wife, Divya Rajya Laxmi Rana, posing with a shot leopard.

Youngest son of Maharaja Juddha Shumsher
J. B. Rana, General Narayan Shumsher, seated
with his wife, Divya Rajya Laxmi Rana, beneath
a painting of his father and four brothers.

KINGDOM PRESENT

February 18, 1951. Cows and sheep grazed peacefully on a flat field behind the temple of Pashupati. Overhead, an unfamiliar droning filled the air. Workers stopped in the rice fields, eyes cast upward. A black spot circled in the sky, then a twin-engine plane swooped down onto an unused landing strip built by the engineers of British India during World War II. With this, the third airplane ever to land in the Kathmandu Valley, came the beginning of a new era. From the aircraft emerged King Tribhuvan, his neck hung with garlands of flowers, returning from a brief exile in India, returning to repossess the Shah power lost to the Ranas a hundred years before.

King Tribhuvan reestablished international diplomatic relations and promised to achieve a democratic government. For the majority of Nepal's people, however, the shift in regimes seemed of little importance. The Kathmandu Valley remained, as always, the seat of power for a few privileged rulers, whose right to rule Nepal had never been seriously challenged by outside ideas.

The Rana compounds were fantasy worlds, no more real to the average person in the Kathmandu Valley or in the surrounding Kingdom of Nepal than an episode of *Dynasty* would be to slum dwellers in an American city. The miniature Buckingham Palaces were walled away behind high gates. The imported European luxuries inside were never seen once they left the backs of the porters who hauled them up long mountain slopes. The occasional dignitaries photographed with fallen tigers and rhinos against backdrops of polished automobiles were rare visitors from the outer world. There were only 360 miles of motor roads in the entire country, and only steep walking trails with their shaky suspension bridges connected Nepal to the outside world. There were no scheduled airline flights. Education was a privilege of the rich, and Nepal's illiteracy rate was a staggering 95.5 percent. Medical care was virtually nonexistent, and the average life expectancy was twenty-six. Two of every ten infants born in Nepal died before the age of five.

Most people of the valley still observed their life rituals as they had for centuries; their education was the legends and tales that had been repeated and

---

The city of Kathmandu sprawls at the foot of the Himalayas.

embellished through the generations. But with the opening of Nepal's borders, the twentieth century crashed in like a tidal wave, merging past with present in shock waves of rapid change—more change within forty years than in two thousand years of changing dynasties.

The valley rapidly opened to the outer world by air and by land. Until 1956 it took sixty-four porters to heave a single automobile up the trade route from India and into the Kathmandu Valley. That year, the first motor road linked the valley to India along the old trading route over the Mahabharat Mountains. Within ten years, a second international highway linked the Kathmandu Valley

Grandson of the late King Tribhuvan, King Birendra Bir Bikram Shah Dev, seen with Queen Aishwarya, now rules and is regarded as a reincarnation of Vishnu. The king and his loyal Army officers watch soldiers perform a khukri knife maneuver during the Ghora Jatra festival.

THIS PAGE AND OPPOSITE

On the first day of spring, known as Basant Panchami, government ministers and military officers join the king of Nepal inside Hanuman Dhoka's Nasal Chowk to witness rites ushering in the season.

Nepalese soldier wearing a traditional topi with crossed khukris.

PAGES 116–18

With more than a million people now living in the Kathmandu Valley, the demand for housing and office space creates jobs for many locals as well as migrant Bengalis in brick factories that seem equal in number to the valley's temples.

with the Tibetan border, and automobiles traversed the trade route from India across the Kathmandu Valley and into China. The world moved closer still in 1974, when the first scheduled international air service began. Today, a network of four thousand miles of roads and forty-three airstrips link the Kathmandu Valley with the Nepal Himalaya. Half a dozen international flights leave from Tribhuvan International Airport each day.

But the most profound change came in the form of foreign aid, beginning with a thousand dollars from the United States in 1951. In the mid 1960s the United Nations declared Nepal the world's fourth poorest country, and money flooded into the country, tripling with each passing decade. With foreign aid came at least enough political reform to appease the international community of givers. There were announced commitments to economic development, human dignity, and human rights. Land reform was enacted in 1951. In 1963, the harsh Hindu caste laws were softened, and representative government, the panchayat system, was established.

The foreign money that poured in to aid the Kingdom of Nepal had a profound impact on health, education, transportation, and communication. Armies of briefcase-carrying foreign aid "experts" arrived in the valley speaking a new vocabulary of buzz words: "aid," "agency," "development," "infrastructure." They turned the area of Pulchowk Hill, near Patan's Durbar Square, into an alpha-

116

bet soup of acronyms: JICA, JOLIC, WHO, UNDP, UNICEF, SATA, GTZ, ISIMOD, CARE.

New prosperity attracted new residents to the valley. Kathmandu's population tripled to more than a million by the end of the 1980s, and the urban area tripled as well, becoming a complex four miles wide and six miles long. A suburbia of modern houses built to the tastes of foreign executives began to transform the traditional landscape of the valley. Land values soared to as much as $55 per square foot for prime commercial property. By 1986, a study by the local town planning office warned that in little more than thirty years, 60 percent of the valley, including the best farmland, would be swallowed by development. Still the building continues, with nearly a hundred brickyards excavating clay in great red gashes to keep up with the demand.

Wealth, meanwhile, remains concentrated in the upper classes. Nepal's average per capita income is $160 per year. Prospects of urban employment keep a steady stream of immigrants pouring into the Kathmandu Valley from the over-populated hill and mountain communities of Nepal, as well as immigrants from the impoverished Gangetic plain of India. Kathmandu's inflation rate is one of the highest in Asia. Even those who hold sought-after government jobs struggle to make ends meet on low salaries. After 1988 cost of living increases, an army field marshall made $200 a month; chief secretary in the government, $190; major general, $170; senior air engineer, $150; police inspector, $100; air mechanic, $65, air hostess, $40; King's Household Cavalryman, $30; army or police recruit, $25.

Development programs have raised the literacy rate in the country from virtually nothing to 33 percent, and health care has improved. Nepal's average life expectancy is now fifty-four for men, fifty-one for women, and child mortality rates have been cut in half. There is now one doctor for every 2,000 residents of the valley, though still only one for every 300,000 outside.

By the standards of most cities, crime in Kathmandu is insignificant, despite a youthful population (half are now under twenty-one), who are struggling to find their identity amid all this change, and a growing drug problem (an estimated 15,000 young heroin addicts). One can still bicycle unmolested by moonlight across the darkened city at midnight. Nevertheless, many art treasures of the valley have been pillaged, and padlocked temples and defaced statues are a sad sign of changing times.

Inevitably, time-honored social customs are also in transition. Marriage is becoming more "westernized," with an increasing number of young couples choosing "love marriages" over the arranged marriages of caste. Young women are discarding saris for knee-length skirts and even jeans. Television antennas protrude from rooftops, video tape rental shops are scattered across the city, and long lines at movie theaters match the crowds at religious festivals. Nepal television offers "Moonlighting" and "Bonanza," although 80 percent of its programs are locally produced. A televised version of the Hindu epic *Ramayana* regularly wins out over other offerings as the top-rated program.

With many grass-roots organizations receiving assistance from development programs, the literacy rate in Nepal has climbed from a mere 5 percent in 1951 to a present rate of 33 percent.

Tourism grew like a twin sister of foreign aid, beginning with Sir Edmund Hillary's climb up Mount Everest in 1953, and attracting a steady and ever-changing stream of outsiders, from mountaineers to hippies to Himalayan trekkers. In the fifties, Boris Lissanevitch, a White Russian former dancer with the Ballets Russes, opened the exclusive Royal Hotel, catering to celebrity clientele. Today, there are 225,000 foreign visitors a year, one for every four residents of the valley, and tourism is Nepal's chief source of income after foreign aid. Kathmandu's half-dozen luxury hotels are but a small wedge in the thick pie of tourism. For most people the cost of a stay in the valley equals the amount of foreign exchange required by the immigration office—five dollars a day—in contrast to the $130-per-day minimum required in neighboring Bhutan.

It was the hippies who arrived in the late sixties who glamorized and romanticized the valley, putting Kathmandu on the Western world's map as a way-out Never-Never Land. Hippies, the disenchanted children of Western civilization, migrated like flocking birds in a perpetual search for the perfect hassle-free utopia of good climate, cheap living, plentiful drugs, and experimental philosophies. By 1963 the first of them arrived in Kathmandu, emerging from dusty buses, long-haired and brilliantly costumed in outfits picked up in countries along the long overland route from Europe, robes of bright silks and cottons, turbans, beads, and sandals. They were ready to be absorbed by anything that seemed to lead toward that undefinable something called "consciousness." Kathmandu, the chosen city, the promised land, Shangri-la, utopia, paradise, did not disappoint.

They found the pastoral landscape a fantasy land of thatched-roofed houses, white stupas, and gilded temple pagodas rising from quiet green fields. New Road, the busiest street in the city, was dead quiet. The hippies made the temples of Durbar Square, Swayambhunath, and Bodhnath their public parks. They strung beads and wrote poetry on the steps of the temples of Durbar Square, sat stoned in the light of the full moon at Swayambhu, played cowboy on the dusty roads of Bodhnath. Jochetol, a side street near Durbar Square, became Freak Street, Main Street of the international counterculture.

Drugs were the route to a new kind of wisdom, and here there were plenty of them—in the 1960s, everything legal—a smorgasbord of grass, hash, opium, LSD, speed, you-name-it stored on long shelves of biscuit tins at corner stores. Hippies turned on beneath murals of Shiva in darkened rooms at the Ling Kasar, the Cabin, the Blue Tibetan, and the Rose Mushroom. They divided into sub-cults, adopting the philosophies of lamas, ascetics, and gurus. The Bouda Bums drank chang and listened to Mick Jagger. The Costo Manches ("What Kind of Man Are You?"), hard-drinking Danes, swaggered along the dusty roads of Bodhnath in cowboy hats. The Happy Skeletons of Swayambhu explored opium and Eastern religions.

The behavior of the hippies held little shock value for the people of the valley, whose primary reaction was a bemused tolerance. No sexual kinkiness could match that already displayed on the ancient temple walls, and the most outlandish hippies couldn't match the religious fervor of the indigenous ascetics.

A swirl of trade around the Annapurna and Ganesh temples swells the open market of Asan Tol, a major stop on the Tibet–Kathmandu–India trading route.

While many hippies disappeared from Kathmandu by the mid 1970s, their heritage, a mom-and-pop tourism industry catering to youthful budget travelers, is still active. From Freak Street to Dharma Path, hippies were welcomed by Newar landlords and transformed the ancient Newar tols of the inner city, where once the highest castes lived, to crash pads that have become today's tourist lodges. And the hippie drug habit led to the munchies, to satisfy which they taught the art of Western pie-making to anyone willing to learn. A row of pie shops sprung up along "pig alley" behind Kasthamandap, which was the beginning of a restaurant industry that transformed Kathmandu from a city with virtually no eating places to a mecca famed across Asia for cheap, edible renditions of Western food. The new immigrants also opened Kathmandu's first book shop, the Spirit Catcher, the beginning of yet another new industry, a thriving trade in used paperback books.

Most of all, the hippies of the 1960s began to walk, to wander up into the hills and mountains, along the ancient trade routes. Today, a major share of Nepal's tourists use Kathmandu as the getting-off place for Himalayan treks.

An orange-colored preservative coats goat heads and other meat for sale in Asan Tol.

A Nepali merchant sells topis, native Nepali hats.

Mobile vegetable seller.

Thamel offers inexpensive accommodations, trekking stores, and a variety of restaurants, which cater to over 200,000 visitors a year.

Exposed to many foreign visitors as well as television and videocassette recordings, many Nepalese are questioning tradition and seeking change.

125

SEASONS
OF THE VALLEY

A blood-red moon poises just above the horizon of the darkened city. It is midnight, and hours ago most lights flickered out. Traffic is but an occasional car or cyclist.

On this New Year's Eve, Kathmandu lies still. The Gregorian calendar and clock of the Western world may run Kathmandu's airlines and its foreign agencies, but not its people. The Western new year is noted only by a few scattered gatherings of Western expatriates singing lonely strains of "Auld Lang Syne." For most people in Kathmandu, the new year is something to celebrate on another day. Tibetans celebrate in February; Nepalis in spring; Newaris in autumn.

Systems of time, like gods, coexist here in comfortable harmony. Western time and Western customs may have gained a certain foothold in business life, but in most ways the Kathmandu Valley still functions on the ancient rhythms of sun, moon, and seasons.

Those seasons are subtle, one flowing into the other with mild temperatures that seldom exceed 86 degrees Fahrenheit, seldom drop below 50 degrees. Each year, sixty inches of rain soak the land; each year the land produces three bountiful harvests. The rotation of crops, plantings, harvests, and the rituals and festivals that accompany them control time more surely than any watch or calendar.

For these reasons, the full moon of this January 1 is fraught with significance. According to the lunar calendar—one of the five systems of time-telling in simultaneous use in the valley—it is time for the completion of an all-important task, the bathing and clothing of a crucial god of agriculture, Seto Machhendranath, in a temple courtyard near Asan Tol.

A dense blanket of fog covers the Kathmandu Valley and its winter wheat.

Early morning on a hillock in a religious forest
on the outskirts of Bhaktapur; such forests are
protected land.

In the chill of winter, a Bhaktapur Newar delivers fresh yogurt to Kathmandu City.

Newar devotees circumambulate Kathmandu's Seto Machhendranath temple. The cult of this idol is one of the oldest and most revered in the valley's religion. The god is identified by the local Buddhists as Avalokitesvara, the Bodhisattva of compassion, and by Hindus as Yamaraja, lord of death. Hindus come to light a candle before the idol when someone in the family is in danger of death. The idol receives a ritual bathing each winter before making its public appearance riding in a rath, or chariot, several weeks later.

OPPOSITE

Newar men construct a four-wheeled chariot, or rath, for pulling Seto Machhendranath around Kathmandu. Locals say the festival was initiated by the Thakuri king Gunakamadev in the tenth century. Each day residents from specific neighborhoods jostle, yank, and tug the lumbering chariot through the narrow streets as devotees make offerings of coins and flowers. Mishaps are common, with the chariot steeple crashing into houses. The communal event lasts for four days, brings the Royal Kathmandu Kumari out for a look, and ends with the chariot circling the shrine of Machhendranath's mother in Langan-khel.

Seto Machhendranath is a white-faced statue, four feet high, with the peaceful expression of a Buddha, an image accorded deep reverence because of its power to bestow long life and fertility, and assure an abundant rice harvest. Twelve days of each winter are devoted to ritual bathing that washes away all the vermilion powder, holy water, milk, honey, blood, and eggs that have been lovingly splattered on the god during the year. Priests have repainted the god's benevolent features and reclothed it in a gleaming tiara, ornate earrings, necklaces, silk brocaded robes, and the sacred thread that all Hindu men wear beneath their clothing.

Such rituals mark the tempo of Kathmandu's seasons. At least one day in three is set aside for some special purpose—living, dying, sowing, reaping, forever worshiping the many gods. Communities come together to create each festival, as a pageant, as a morality play with instructive lessons from the gods, or merely as a welcome break from the daily routine. Each festival offers its own reality, with familiar characters who appear year after year, like a soap opera that began deep in the past. As the images of Kathmandu's many gods are hoisted and tugged through city streets from one holy site to another, they come to life, reinforcing their cosmic powers.

Festivals often continue for a fortnight and sometimes an entire lunar month. The cycle of festivals is so attuned to the waxing and waning of the moon that astrologers are required to establish their exact dates. The pace of festival life quickens in agricultural lulls, slows to meet the demands of planting and harvest.

Seto Machhendranath is a white-faced statue
whose style is believed to have been derived
from the Lichhavi Kings of the fourth through
ninth centuries.

ABOVE

Newari priests transport the serene Seto Machhendranath idol to the rath while hundreds of
devotees offer oil lamps in Asan Tol square.

WINTER

Winter is a quiet time. A chill settles each evening and, by early morning, becomes a dense blanket of fog, shrouding the landscape in ghostly grays and whites. Figures loom in the mist. If the cold seems intense, it is not so much a matter of temperature as the inadequacy of defenses against it. Nature's seasons are accepted as they come. Houses are heated only by small cooking fires or pots of hot coals. Indoor plumbing and the further luxury of hot water are something few families can afford. On the coldest mornings, women wrap themselves in woolen shawls, but walk with bare feet or sandals on cold stones. Men wear hats and neck scarves, but seldom jackets or closed shoes.

On most winter days the pale disk of the sun appears on the surface of the gray sky at mid morning. Within minutes the fog vanishes and the chill of winter burns away. The sky brightens to clear blue, and the sun warms the earth anew, highlighting the white snow peaks on the horizon and the subtle colors of the winter landscape, hillsides tinted in the greens and golds of budding wheatfields and mustard crops.

There are fifty days of winter, and the thirty of them that fall in the Nepali month of Poush are considered unlucky, a time to avoid any new enterprise, including marriage and household moves. But the winter sun changes all that the day it moves toward the northern hemisphere, Magh Sakranti. Though it is often the year's coldest day, it is the one deemed most beneficial for ritual bathing. At dawn, Nepali men, women, and children venture through the fog to the banks of the holy Bagmati. The full moon that follows holds particular significance for women as the beginning of a month devoted to the study of religious texts and fasting in honor of the god Shiva.

By early February, two kinds of pilgrims begin to appear on the streets of the valley, converging from the north and from the south.

Wearing heavy woolens and yak-hide boots, the inhabitants of the cold hills to the north descend to the valley, to the stupa of Bodhnath. They are a sturdy, heavy-boned people, wind-chapped faces carved with deep wrinkles. The annual pilgrimage to Kathmandu is an opportunity to trade and attend the festival of Losar, the Tibetan New Year, as well as to study with the great masters of Tibetan Buddhism who inhabit the valley. The hill people join a procession of Tibetan Buddhists circling the stupa clockwise, following the path of the sun, spinning prayer wheels to send the eternal mantra, *om mani padme hum*, into the heavens. The most devout inch in a slow circle around the stupa, prostrating their bodies, forearms extended, rubbing away the skin of their foreheads in repeated abrasions against the cold stone.

On Magh Sakranti (during January–February) the sun changes its course and begins to "move" toward the northern hemisphere. Despite the penetrating cold, this day is deemed most beneficial for ritual bathing. Many men and women gather along the banks of the sacred Bagmati River, notably in Patan's Sankhamole area, to launch leaf-plate offerings of burning butter wicks while praising their gods and petitioning blessings.

During Magh (January) many devout Hindu
men and women observe a month-long fast and
study the Swastani text explaining creation and
the feats of Shiva (in the guise of Mahadev) and
Vishnu (as Narayan), who brought peace to the
suffering. Wearing white cotton wraps, symbolic
color of purity, foreheads dabbed with vermilon
paste blessings, these Hindu boys go through the
streets of Sanku, giving blessings to the
villagers.

Men and women gather together at the Narayan temple in Sankhu to spend a month studying religious texts and fasting in honor of Shiva's wife, Parvati. It was her month-long fast and devotion that won Shiva.

Shiva Ratri is a twenty-four-hour adoration of Lord Shiva, the god of destruction in the Hindu triad and one of the valley's most revered deities. The golden-tiered Pashupatinath temple is dedicated to Shiva as lord of the animals and Nepal's patron god. The entire area has numerous shrines, bathing and cremation ghats, and scattered stone sculptures including the devoutly worshiped Shiva lingam. Throughout the year, Pashupatinath attracts sadhus (ascetics), mendicants, and other devotees, but on the festival day thousands of pilgrims arrive to take a purifying bath in the sacred Bagmati River and then pay homage to the sacred lingam inside the main Pashupatinath temple. Throughout the day and well into the night, one can witness ash-covered sadhus, foreheads painted with tridents, emulating Lord Shiva by performing various yoga feats. Mahashiva Ratri is also a time for many Shivite followers to debate the great Hindu texts.

Brilliant dye powders used in Shiva Ratri and other festivals.

From the south come frail, barefoot men and women wrapped in thin cotton saris, loincloths, and drawstring pants, balancing large bundles on their heads and backs. Their clothing is too light for the chilly winter evenings, poor even by the standards of this land where poverty is often visible. But their eyes are bright, reflecting a fevered inner light. They are Hindu pilgrims bound for Pashupatinath to celebrate Shiva Ratri, Lord Shiva's night. If the long foot journey from the plains of India was difficult, all the better, for it will bring merit in the next life.

By mid February the waning moon is a sliver overhead. Pashupatinath has become a mass of humanity, a carnival mob bumping elbows as they bathe in the Bagmati River, crunching into long lines at temple entrances with their puja offerings, striving to obey Shiva's dictate: "Those who fast on the fourteenth day of the moon in February in honor of my lingam, who that night do puja and present me with the leaves of the margosa shall be certain of a place in Mount Kailash."

There are mingled smells of burning wood, burning flesh, burning cow dung, sweat, incense, and marijuana. There is a cacophony of sound, flutes, drums, stringed instruments, bells, cymbals, and the murmur of hundreds and thousands of human voices. People seem costumed, rather than clothed, their foreheads tikkaed with bright-colored powders, daubed with rice, flower petals, and holy water. There are women in bright saris, turbaned men, and countless beggars thrusting the stumps of maimed limbs to demand alms.

Bands of rhesus monkeys frolic, and cows wander, dropping dung that is immediately scooped up and, after drying, offered to the gods.

Hawkers vend a plethora of items with which one can please and appease the gods—bright powders, garlands of flowers, rudraksha beads, oil, incense,

fruits, sweets, musical instruments, and much more. It is a visual feast, full of the joy of festival and the despair of life, and the sadhus, ascetic pilgrims from India, are the main course. They huddle in groups to inhale marijuana from clay pipes, uttering *bam shankar,* "I am Shiva." Technically, it is illegal to smoke dope in Nepal, but the heady smell that fills the air is ignored by police this one day of the year. The god Shiva smoked dope to gain spiritual insight, and the sadhus do likewise.

They also imitate Shiva's ascetic form, smearing their bodies in ghostly white ashes. Their long hair is tangled, matted in snakelike strands that symbolize the chaos of the world. They fast, eyes bright from hunger, red from dope and lack of sleep. Every three hours they descend to the river to wash their feet. Agore babas, a subcaste of sadhus, entertain tourists with bizarre feats of endurance that demonstrate their ability to transcend pain.

Lasting for one week, Losar marks the New Year for all Tibetan and Bhotia peoples in Nepal. It is the best time to see the great melange of Himalayan Buddhist peoples dressed in their traditional garb. In the Tibetan gompas Lamas and monks perform a week-long Mahakala ritual to abolish the accumulated impurities of the preceding year. On the fourth day, great crowds gather at the Bodhanath stupa to offer Buddhist prayer flags to be strung over the width of the stupa. The offer brings merit to the individual and his family. A procession of monks carries an image of the Dalai Lama, Tibetan Buddhism's temporal and spiritual leader, around the stupa. The ceremony ends with a blast of long horns followed by the hurling of tsampa—powdered grain—into the air for good luck.

Less than a week after Shiva Ratri, the Tibetan festivities at Bodhnath reach their climax on Losar, the Tibetan New Year.

Kathmandu's permanent Tibetan community began to form in 1959, when the People's Republic of China annexed Tibet, unleashing an exodus of refugees into India and Nepal. Now a community of more than ten thousand, many Tibetans have grown prosperous from their thriving carpet industry, which has become Nepal's largest foreign-exchange earner after tourism. The Tibetan community centers at Jawalakhel and Bodhnath, the stupa where Tibetan travelers of past centuries traditionally paused to worship when traversing the long trade route toward India.

On the third day of Losar, the sun shines bright on the stupa, which is strung with prayer flags bearing formulas for success in the new year. Adversity has been conquered with the burning of effigies, and now the fragrant smell of burning juniper leaves and herbs fills the air. Hundreds of people gather on the stupa steps before pictures of the Dalai Lama, repeating a chant that grows louder

and louder into a vast buzzing *"ommmmm."*

At a moment as precise as the descent of the ball at midnight in New York's Times Square, clouds of rice and tsampa, a powdered grain, are thrown into the air for good luck, and the shout, *Lha gya lo!*—"May the gods be victorious!"—reverberates.

The new year begun, it is time to drink and dance the afternoon away. There is only good fortune to expect in the year to come. The elements of luck are dispensed freely to anyone who does so much as wander into a courtyard. Boisterous celebrants pour glasses of chang, a milk-white barley beer, and offer sweets, the symbol of good luck and prosperity. Families picnic, dance, sing, and watch performances of traditional Tibetan opera.

OPPOSITE

Bodhanath stupa glowing on a full-moon night.

150

WEST MEETS EAST

The shop just outside the entrance of Bodhnath advertises "Dharma Books." Inside, a monk browses, wearing a burgundy robe. His head is shaved bald, but when he turns, his face is young, eyebrows blond, eyes a brilliant blue. It is yet another Western student of Buddhism, not an uncommon sight around the stupa.

In the late eighties they began to arrive, transforming Bodhnath into a kind of Buddhist University. In a way, it is a fulfillment of the quest for consciousness begun by the hippies of the sixties. But the quest, if it *is* the same quest, has turned from self-indulgence and drug-taking to the opposite extreme, the Buddhist ideal of total control.

Western Buddhist converts like to quote the ancient Tibetan prophecy: "When the iron bird flies in the sky, the Dharma will go West."

The movement centers around a Tibetan monk named Chokyi Nyima Rinpoche, whose age, thirty-eight, would make him a baby boomer if his birth had been in the West. As a child, he was proclaimed to be an incarnate lama, a realized being with a mind as old as the valley, among the wisest of the living. Chokyi Nyima counsels about fifty Western students of Buddhism each day, many of whom live in Kathmandu primarily to absorb his teachings.

He is an unpretentious man, sitting on a plaid Danish modern sofa in a large, calm room furnished with Tibetan rugs, golden Buddhas, silver bowls of holy water, and a photograph of the Dalai Lama. Around him red-robed monks kneel on the polished wood floor. The smell of incense rises into the air as a young couple from Boston, new arrivals to the valley, enter to kneel at the rinpoche's feet and proclaim, "We have sold our house and come here to practice."

A barefoot boy monk serves the visitors a tray of Coca-Cola and Sprite, and they listen reverently as he speaks:

"Buddhism is 99 percent about insight into the nature of people and things. For people who are interested in those things I can say a lot. Buddha taught that everything is impermanent. That's simple to understand. Holding onto transient things brings pain. The root of all disturbing emotions is ego. When people discover this for themselves they are happy."

Chokyi Nyima Rinpoche

Nearby, Kathryn, a follower in faded jeans and a pink sweat shirt, waits to see the rimpoche.

"Chokyi Nyima has a profound effect on people, which goes beyond what you see or hear," she observes. "What he says is almost always simple and direct and cuts through the complications we make for ourselves. That kind of simplicity and directness is becoming rare these days. When I walk into a Western church it is if something has been washed away. Westerners are goal-oriented to this life rather than thinking of responsibility for the future. A lot of people there prefer not to know what happens after death.

"It's impossible to leave Kathmandu if you're here and know what's here. It's a Vatican city of the East. You're surrounded by realized beings. Life in Bodhnath is the perfect expression of Buddha's teachings."

Tibetan Buddhism's most learned teacher, H. H. Dilgo Khyentse Rinpoche, blessing a close friend.

SPRING

The morning fogs of winter end in late February. Now long days of sunshine bring the earth—and those who live on it—to life. People smile, birds warble, new-born lambs gambol. Occasional afternoon showers refresh the landscape. The wheat, mustard, and other crops of the terraced hills turn from pale winter tints to bright greens and yellows. Blossoms splash the landscape with yellows, reds, blues, purples, oranges.

ABOVE

A young Chhetrini weeds a mustard field.

OPPOSITE

After a few spring showers, vibrant green wheat fields with patches of yellow mustard cover the valley's landscape.

LEFT

Jacaranda trees burst into flower in downtown Kathmandu.

PAGES 156–57

Newar and Chhetri women weed mustard plants and a buckwheat field. The mustard plant will be squeezed for cooking oil and the buckwheat, once dried, ground into flour for making flat bread and a thick, pasty staple called dhido.

Willows line the Manohara River in which a
woman washes bundles of onions to be sold in
Kathmandu.

Winter and early spring is also the time of weddings. Countless processions wind through the streets each night to the tempo of discordant melodies played by bands of musicians blowing brass horns. Rented white sedans follow, decorated with colored strips of crepe paper. Brides ride in back seats, veiled heads dipped in embarrassment.

The marriage ceremonies of Kathmandu still have a medieval quality. Most marriages are arranged by fathers between children of the same caste and social standing, and few brides and grooms meet before the ceremony. Weddings are seasonal, the auspicious date set according to careful astrological calculations, and they go on for days, involving elaborate rituals. In season, the price of gold leaps—the necessary dowry of an upper-class bride, though even the poorest goes to her husband adorned with gilded ornaments.

In Western terms, Nepalese traditions of marriage are harsh. A woman must almost certainly marry; the Nepalese inheritance system passes property from father to son. Only in the absence of a son does a daughter inherit wealth. A bride must live with her husband's family, obeying the dictates of her mother-in-law. If she follows the strictest traditions of orthodox Hindu castes, she will have to wash her husband's feet each morning, then drink the water. But the bride's father will drink her bath water when she returns home, for in marriage, she has become a goddess. A widowed woman, no matter how young, faces social ostracism if she remarries, for her bad luck caused the first husband's death.

Spring brings a curious ceremony known as Ihi, the wedding of prepubescent Newari girls, six to ten years old, to the god Narayan. The ceremony is a creative Newar reaction to the Hindu marriage laws imposed on them in the Licchavi era. If a girl is married to a god first and a mortal husband second, the husband's death won't necessitate submission to the harsh Hindu laws of widowhood.

The groom attends the wedding in the form of the fruit of the wood-apple tree, the bya, a green fruit that somewhat resembles a pear. At ten o'clock on a morning in early spring, sixty-seven Newar girls marry their bya-fruit gods at a courtyard near Durbar Square. Clad in reds and gold brocade, they sit cross-legged upon the dusty gray stones around a wood fire burning on a brick platform. A red ruffled canopy is suspended above the brides, separating them from the prosaic world overhead, where laundry flaps from apartment windows and pigeons march in a line across a tile roof.

Each girl's forehead is daubed with the same vermilion powder that a human groom will someday put there. Dark eyes outlined in black kohl shine with anticipation. Dark hair is tied back with red bows and adorned with red flowers. Toenails gleam with red polish, and wrists tinkle with red bangle bracelets.

The long ritual progresses slowly, with scatterings of flower petals and the eating of fruits and sweets from a plate of symbolic offerings in front of each bride. Finally, a chanting priest places the bya fruit into each plate, and the bride's father binds her hand with its leaves. After the ceremony, the bya fruit is kept safe from harm on the roof of the house, for if it is crushed or broken, the girl's mortal husband will die and leave her a widow.

Ihi ceremony, in which prepubescent Newari girls symbolically marry Narayan in the form of the *bya* (fruit of the wood-apple tree). If a girl is married to a god first and a mortal husband second, the death of the husband won't force her into observance of the strict Hindu laws of widowhood. The ceremony involves a series of purification rituals, including the placing of sindoor (vermilion) in the part of the girl's hair as a sign of marriage.

In mid April comes the third significant New Year of the Kathmandu Valley, the first day of the Nepalese solar calendar. A peculiar form of New Year's Eve takes place in Bhaktapur. Bisket is a celebration of victory over the snake gods that ruled the valley in the time of prehistory. It is believed that most of the nagas, or snake gods, evacuated the Kathmandu Valley with the prehistoric draining of its great lake, but a few remained, great serpent kings dwelling in the rivers and the ponds, wielding that most significant of powers, control over rainfall.

On Bisket, "snake slaughter," all the spirits of the gods descend on Bhaktapur, where an eighty-foot lingam carved from a tree stands fluttering with banners. The banners represent two serpent demons slaughtered by a Malla prince when they emerged from the nostrils of a sleeping princess.

Crowds follow a procession of two heavy chariots, one carrying Bhairav, the wrathful form of Shiva; the other Badra Kali, the bloodthirsty form of Shiva's wife Parvati. The crowd divides into teams for a tug of war between the chariots. The winners will have good luck in the coming year. Finally, more straining teams compete to bring the giant lingam to earth. The moment it crashes, the old year dies, and so do the snake demons. The Nepalese new year begins.

During April's nine-day New Year festival in Bhaktapur, residents from the east and west sides of town stage a frenzied tug-of-war, pulling a huge chariot containing the Hindu deity Bhairab. Later, the chariot is hauled to an open area near the Hanumante River, where an eighty-foot pole is erected, adorned with two banners representing serpents, only to be felled the next day to mark the beginning of the new year. Throughout the day, Bhaktapur residents offer live fowl for sacrifice to the bloodthirsty Hindu deity, Badrakali.

Three miles west of Bhaktapur, in the village of Thimi, New Year is celebrated by men carrying all the neighborhood deity images through the narrow streets in *khats;* the men finally assemble with the images in front of the Bal Kumari temple. Devotees fling fistful of orange powder over everyone as a blessing for the New Year.

Three miles west of Bhaktapur, at the village of Thimi, the new year is celebrated late into the night with the burning of hundreds of ceremonial oil torches so hot they drive away the last of winter and bring warm days of sunshine to nourish the crops. On the second day of the new year, neighborhood deities are carried through the street in temple-like wooden structures called khats. Spectators shower the images and one another with orange powder. To soak one's friends and neighborhood in dye powder is a token of good wishes and respect, just as it is to honor gods and goddesses.

Across the highway from Thimi is the village of Bode, which has its own new year procession and another ceremony, a tongue boring at the temple of the goddess Mahalaxmi. A volunteer, who has undergone a four-day cleansing ceremony, offers himself to the temple pujari, who holds the man's extended tongue with a piece of cloth. The pujari thrusts a long, spikelike needle through the penitent's tongue, and the man walks about the village so that all may witness the penance. Bleeding is considered an ill omen; a bloodless penance is seen as evidence of great merit.

An abundant rice harvest requires the heavy rains of the monsoon, falling in torrents, day and night for three months, turning the soil to oozing mud from which tender green rice shoots emerge, grow, and ripen. If the snake gods are not happy, they will not release the rain. Once, they were imprisoned, which caused a twelve-year drought and great famine, until the god Rato Machhendranath released them, restoring the rains and thus the prosperity of the valley.

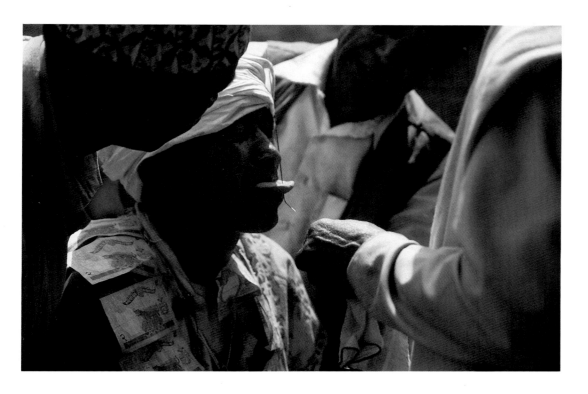

In Bode village, every New Year a man volunteers to fast twenty-four hours and then stand on a stage to have his tongue bored with a thin steel spike. He walks through the village, the spike in place, and carries around a disklike trellis, with flaming torches along the rim. In return for such a performance, it is believed, the man will go straight to Heaven when he dies.

Rato Machhendranath, popularly known as Bungadeo, is the Patan prototype of Kathmandu's Seto Machhendranath. During the summer months, the idol lives in Bungmati, two kilometers south of Patan, and the rest of the year in Patan's Tahbahal. Rato Machhendranath is the chief deity for all Newar Jyapus in the valley. Historical records refer to the chariot festival as early as the ninth century, making it the oldest festival in the valley. In a manner similar to the chariot festival of Seto Machhendranath in Kathmandu, the Rato Machhendranath chariot is pulled through Patan's four localities: Gabahal, Sundhara, Lagankhel, and Jawalakhel. With each stop residents celebrate and make offerings of burning oil lamps. In some places, an individual representing the area lies down with burning oil lamps placed over his body to gain merit for his locality.

Machhendranath, who was born a prince in Assam, had a younger brother, Gorakhanath, born from cow dung, who came to Nepal as a yogi begging for alms, but he found no donors. Distressed, he tied the rain-giving nagas (snake gods) together, causing a terrible drought. Only Machhendranath could free the snake gods. A tantric priest from Kathmandu and a porter from Patan were sent to summon the god, who came to Nepal as a bee and was trapped in a vase in Bungmati. After arguments between the king and the porter about where the god should live, it was decided that he would spend time in each place. Hence Rato Machhendranath's two homes. Gorakhanath was persuaded to free the snake gods, yielding the necessary rain for the valley rice to grow. To this day, Machhendranath is revered as the compassionate one and is propitiated to bring the monsoon rains. Before Rato Machhendranath leaves Patan for Bungmati, the king of Nepal as well as the Patan kumari come to pay their respects.

The red sister image of the white-faced Seto Machhendranath, Rato Machhendranath came to the valley in the form of a bee imprisoned in a vase, a vessel painted with the image of the god and enshrined at the village of Bungamati as the god of rain and harvest. During the festival of Rato Machhendranath, the five-foot vase is carefully bathed and repainted at its temple near Patan's Durbar Square.

The cult of Rato Machhendranath is older than that of any other god worshiped in the valley. Indeed, the cults devoted to the other gods derived from this one, and, today, only the Machhendranath festival draws people from all parts of the valley; all the other festivals tend to be more strictly local. Rato Machhendranath—whose real name is Bunga-daya (Machhendranath is used when speaking to non-Newars)—has the further distinction of being the only deity of the valley who has two temples of residence.

At Pulchowk Hill, near one of the ancient Ashoka stupas, workers carve a chariot from gigantic timbers, with massive wooden wheels and a great front beam shaped like a serpent head. It towers fifty feet high. Machhendranath is placed in his chariot, and hundreds of men heave it a few hundred yards each day, while crowds of people gather alongside. There, on a designated day, the crowd grows into a vast mob. Both the living goddess of Patan and the king of Nepal arrive to watch the priest emerge to show them the waistcoat of the deity, a gift from the snake gods.

In a long torchlight procession, Rato Machhendranath is carried to the village of Bungamati to begin the new agricultural year.

SUMMER

Now big festivals cease, and the people of the valley begin the serious task of planting rice. There is one last day of worship to appease the snake gods. Naga Pancham protects houses from damage by the heavy rains that will surely come. If a house sinks into the oozing mud of a rice field, it is not the heavy floods undermining the foundation, it is the unhappy snake gods, writhing in their discontent.

In June clouds blow in from the east, and the monsoon rains begin, all night and most of the day. The sky turns an ominous gray, and even during the few hours the sun shines, the air is so heavy with humidity that a spoonful of dry salt will turn to salt water within a few hours. Plants shoot forth as lush and luxuriant as in a tropical rain forest.

As with the winter chill, most people do little to defend themselves against nature's onslaught, adopting an attitude of "ke garne," a familiar Nepali expression that translates "What to do?" Most simply find a spot to stand beneath the eaves of a building or under a tree until the rain stops. Those who must venture out wrap themselves in a sheet of plastic. Travel slows to a near halt. Dirt roads become swamps. Asphalt roads crumble. Low city streets flood. Rice fields become lakes. Highways are blocked by mudslides.

For many, monsoon is a time of sickness. The rain washes sewage into the water supplies, bringing epidemics of typhoid, hepatitis, and other water-borne diseases. Yet, despite nature's obstacles, communities band together to plant new crops of rice. They work in the unrelenting rain, wearing makeshift umbrellas of bamboo and leaves.

The first signs that monsoon is ending appear at certain crossroads on an afternoon in late August. There one finds leafy crosses, bowls of food for the gods, and children blocking roads with rope, demanding tolls for passage. The rains still pour, but a new round of festivals begins with this celebration of the death of Ghanta Karna, devil rival of the good Lord Vishnu.

For all high-caste Hindu men, another kind of new year is commemorated on the full moon of late August with the changing of their sacred thread, a triple strand of yellow cotton string worn beneath the clothing as a symbol of body, speech, and mind. On this same day, throngs of people crush into a square in Kumbeshwar, Patan, where a holy lingam has been placed into a square pond. Boys dive and swim in the pond, and the devout line up to make pujas to the water. For the donation of a few paisa, a priest will tie a yellow string about the wrist and bless it with a quick prayer. After three months, the string must be tied to the tail of a sacred cow, to help your soul pass through the gates of judgment.

To the unschooled eye, the sacred cows of Kathmandu are no more unique than Borden's Elsie. The lumbering brown-and-black creatures roam loose in the streets, creating chaos in urban traffic by choosing to sleep on busy intersections and walk straight into moving vehicles. Cows are protected by the government.

A Chhetri man finds company with the elephant god Ganesh while he waits out a monsoon rain.

169

Villagers work in the spirit of togetherness as they transplant rice shoots.

The death of a cow brings an inquest with potential penalties on a par with manslaughter. For just as the virgin Kumari is the goddess Taleju, just as the king of Nepal is the god Vishnu, the cow is likewise a deity, Mahalaxmi. Milk and all its products—cream, curd, and cheese—are revered, and more often offered to the gods by the devout than consumed.

One of the particular benefits the cow goddess can bestow is a kind of ticket to heaven. Due to her status as deity, a cow can walk straight through the gates of judgment on the one day each year when they are opened. She walks past Yama Raj, the god of death who records all mortal births, deaths, and good and bad deeds in his ledger. Those who cling to the cow's tail likewise can enter. There is, conveniently, a festival to facilitate this, Gai Jatra. *Gai* means cow, and *jatra* is the name applied to any festival in which a decorated idol is carried in procession.

Processions thread through city streets, sometimes led by a living cow tikkaed and adorned with bright flowers, sometimes a cow effigy made of papier-mâché, attended by musicians blowing horns, clashing cymbals, and beating drums. Malla kings once kept a census of deaths by counting the processions.

In mid September women of all ages crowd into the temple of Pashupatinath, excited and giggling, dressed in red marriage saris, adorned with the gold jewelry of their dowries. It is the festival of Tij Brata, three days that reenact the rituals of Parvati, wife of Shiva. Parvati fasted, meditated, and performed rites of absolution to win the notice of her god-husband, and the women of the Kathmandu Valley now do the same.

This one festival strictly for women is to assure a happy marriage, children, purification of body and soul, and long life—for the husband. In the framework of this patriarchal society, such blessings are a woman's own. Eyes bright with hunger from a twenty-four-hour fast, the women dance and make offerings to Pashupati, smothering the holy lingam with gifts and garlands of flowers, drinking holy Bagmati water, making countless pujas to Shiva and Parvati. At home, wives carefully tend the flame of an oil lamp, keeping it alight through the night to assure the husband's long life. They bathe his feet and touch their foreheads reverently to his toes.

In the dark early-morning hours of the third day of Tij, women congregate at the junction of the holy Bagmati and Vishnumati rivers to perform a centuries-old ritual of bathing. Clustered temples and viharas of crumbling bricks and cracking wood stand at the river's edge, adorned with stone deities smeared with vermilion, dotted with clinging flower petals. The bathing process is time-consuming and exact: red mud smeared 360 times on body parts, including between legs; teeth brushed 360 times with the leaves of a certain sacred shrub, the datiwan. (360 is once for each day of the year the ritual was neglected.) Once purified by the ritual, a woman is absolved of sin, including that attached to the awful taboo of having touched a man while menstruating.

By ten A.M., only a few bathers remain in the water. Rings of women sit shielded from the morning sun beneath black umbrellas, feasting on sweets and rice served up in dishes made of palm fronds.

On this day, the god of death, Yama, opens the gates of judgment. The Newars believe that the soul of the deceased wanders through hazards, accompanied only by a cow, until this day when the soul can travel on to its next life guided by the cow. Thus, on the opening day of Gai Jatra, families who have suffered a death in the previous year parade a cow or cow effigy through the streets.

Tij is a festival in which upper-caste women reenact the myth of Parvati's fast for Shiva. While Lord Shiva was grieving over the death of his wife, the demon world was gaining power over the gods. Needing a warrior to defeat the demons, the gods breathed life back into Shiva's wife, who was sent as Parvati to seduce Shiva. Shiva, however, was unmoved by her beauty. Only after she had fasted away almost to nothing did Shiva take notice, fall in love, and marry her. Their son Kumar was born, and he defeated the demons.

On the night before the fast, women gorge themselves on food until midnight. The following morning, dressed in their best, usually red wedding saris, they go to the banks of the Bagmati River to perform ablutions, which include biting the sacred datiwan plant. Next, they perform dances, reenacting the dance Parvati performed for Shiva. On the next day, women break their fast by washing their husband's feet and drinking the water.

In late September there is another celebration of womanhood, the week of Indra Jatra, when Kathmandu's Royal Kumari is paraded through the city streets to bless neighborhoods and bestow the tikka of renewed power on the king, who bows at her feet.

The Royal Kumari is something of a tourist attraction, a face familiar from the covers of guidebooks and picture postcards. Her eyes shine with the engaging quality of the remarkably photogenic. Her young girl's face is a dual study in sensuality and innocence, a face of contrasts. The flawless skin is accentuated by lips and forehead painted a brilliant red. Her hair and eyes are ebony black, while her ears and neck gleam with gold and silver. Garlands of yellow flowers drape about her neck, and at the center of the mask painted on her forehead is a single black-and-gold eye, the omniscient third eye of the goddess Taleju.

A most alluring celebrity, she lives cloistered in her house at Durbar Square, to be seen only in fleeting glimpses framed by an intricately carved window of the Kumari House, or, on rare occasions such as Indra Jatra, seated high in her chariot. The Kumari does not attend school. The goddess has private tutors. She has never shed blood, not from cut, scratch, or menstruation, and once her vigilant attendant, the Kumarina, informs the king's advisers of the loss of so much as a drop of blood, her body will be declared deserted by the goddess, reduced in status to that of an ordinary mortal.

There are nine other kumaris in the Kathmandu Valley, but only this one holds the power of the Kingdom of Nepal in her hands. No king since the eighteenth century has ruled without her blessing. In 1954, a sleepy Kumari accidentally tikkaed the crown prince Mahendra instead of King Tribhuvan; the king died within months, and the prince ascended to the throne.

Hours before the Kumari's chariot ride, a crowd begins to gather in Durbar Square, filling every foot of space, every pyramiding step of every temple within sight of Kumari House. The courtyards of the palaces are adorned with the icons of Indra Jatra. A fifty-foot pine tree is spattered and sanctified with sacrificial blood. There are images of Indra on high scaffolds, outstretched arms bound like those of a thief, and masks of the wrathful Bhairav beneath elaborate canopies draped with flowers. For Indra, the rain god, once took mortal form to pick white blossoms in the valley, was imprisoned as a thief, then apologetically released and fêted. In return, he granted the valley its "milk," the blanket of fog that hovers over the land to moisten the plants during the otherwise dry winter months.

A military rifle squad fires volleys, and a goat is sacrificed on the yoke of the Kumari's chariot to assure a safe voyage. Carefully, the goddess child is carried to the chariot, her feet held high above the spiritually polluted earth, which she must not touch. The great wheels turn, painted with the same lotus eyes as the valley's great Buddhist stupas. Weaving through the dark streets of the city, the Kumari sits on her chariot throne with all the poise of a queen.

It was such poise that had caused her selection in the first place, as well as her beauty, which conforms to the following criteria:

A fierce, red-masked Lakhe demon dancer performs at Indra Jatra.

Kathmandu Kumari

Patan Kumari

Body like a banyan tree
Feet and hands [veined] like a duck's
Thighs like a deer's
Chest like a lion's
Neck like a conch shell
Round head with a cone-shaped top
Voice clear and soft like a duck's
Eyelashes like a cow's

When chosen at age three, the Kumari has to prove her divinity through perfect composure under stress. She is cast down in a dark dungeon filled with the severed heads of animals and ghoulish noises. That she shows no fear is considered evidence that her body is inhabited by a superior soul. In other respects, the selection process is not unlike a Western beauty pageant, in which the winning girl combines poise with beauty, keeping her cool under hot lights, cameras, and the stares of the audience, hiding all emotions behind a rigid smile.

THE BHAKTAPUR KUMARI

Quedar, the high priest of the Taleju temple of Bhaktapur, dodges through narrow city streets lined with cracked, leaning buildings. He dips his head to stoop through a tiny doorway, strides across a couple of trash-strewn courtyards and into the Vihar temple, where the Kumari of Bhaktapur has granted an audience.

Quedar's stature in the ancient hierarchy of Brahmin caste is considerable, for only he can enter the cloistered chambers of Bhaktapur's patron goddess, Taleju. But his priestly mysticism seems to end with the red tikka mark smeared on his forehead. A t-shirt outlines a paunch belly suspended comfortably over beige polyester slacks. He wears glasses and a wristwatch, has neatly clipped hair, a stubble of beard growing on his double chin, and a felt-tip pen in his shirt pocket. Though the strictest of customs forbids him physical contact with "polluted" Westerners who smoke and eat beef, he gives us a hearty handshake. Old laws don't always apply in the changing world of the valley.

The Kumari enters, a little girl seated on a throne of wood. Her forehead is a red triangle outlined in yellow. Her black eyes are outlined seductively in black kohl, her ears adorned with gold loops, her wrists with red plastic bangle bracelets. She does not speak or smile, but simply waits. Passive, shy, controlled, her eyes betray no curiosity, and the only trace of emotion is revealed in the slight pulsation of her throat.

The temple guardian, her attendant, is an old man with missing front teeth, his chin covered in a scraggle of beard, dressed in ragged white cottons with gray cap and vest. He puts a garland of flowers around the neck of the goddess, flowers in her hair, then squats on the concrete floor.

The high priest bows low and places a plate of offerings at the feet of the goddess, a cluster of bananas and some oil-soaked yellow pastry topped with chocolate frosting.

The Kumari remains mute as photographs are taken and questions are asked, though the throat pulsates harder and, finally, the eyes begin to rove restlessly. Even goddesses get tired when they are only nine years old.

FALL

The Kumari is an incarnation of Taleju, who is one of the many manifestations of the goddess Durga, to whom a massive animal sacrifice is made during the festival of Dasain, a few weeks after Indra Jatra. Dasain is a ten-day sadhana—act of worship—a prayer to Durga, the mother earth goddess; the festival also celebrates the victory of the black, ten-armed Durga over Mahisasura, a ferocious water buffalo demon who terrorized the earth—a triumph of good over evil. Preparations are intense. People meticulously clean and repaint their houses. They collect a holiday pay bonus from employers and crowd into stores to buy new clothing and gifts, as well as temple offerings for the gods. Shops and government offices close for an entire week. The city streets fill with herds of animals, sheep, goats, ducks, chickens, and water buffalo, destined to die on a sacrificial altar. And, wherever possible, ingenious swings, called pings, are erected with bamboo and rope. They dot the landscape—and provide rare opportunities for boys and girls to flirt.

In the Kathmandu Valley—as elsewhere in the world—Fall is the time of harvest as well as the time to celebrate harvest. A dense, milky fog settles on the terraced valley below Kokonah, a sixteenth-century Newari village south of Patan. A Hindu temple to the village patroness, Rudrayani, one of the mother goddesses, dominates the center of the village. Kokonah is known for its fine mustard oil.

With the great harvest celebration of Dasain, anticipated with the same eagerness as Christmas is in the West, communally made bamboo swings—pings—are erected all over the valley.

On each night of Dasain, a group of dancers, the Asta Matrikas—eight mother earth goddesses, protectors of ten different directions, subduers of obstacles—weave through the dark streets of Patan, faces covered in jeweled masks representing eight faces of the goddess Durga. Just as images take on the power of gods, the dancers' bodies are believed to be inhabited by the goddesses they portray, inspiring a frenzied dance to the beat of throbbing drums.

Animal sacrifice has always been an important part of the valley's religious rituals, and until this century even human sacrifice was practiced at certain temples, most notably the one in the town of Harisiddhi. There the birthday of Kumar, warrior son of Shiva, was celebrated with a rock fight between two teams of boys; the injured losers were put to death on sacrificial altars. The practice was abolished in 1870.

In Patan's Mul Chowk during Dasain's Navratri (ninth night) Asta Matrika dancers celebrate the goddess Durga's triumph over the buffalo demon Mahisasura. Men and boys dressed to represent the mother-earth goddess become possessed with the goddess's energy and perform acts showing her powers. The performances were initiated in the seventeenth century by the Malla king Srinivasa, whose father built the Krishna temple in Patan.

Indrani dances in an orange mask covered with eyes; nobody can hide from the goddess. Maheswari dances in a white mask, which represents the female aspect of Shiva, who continually combats demons. Brahmayani, in a yellow mask, represents the human aspect of Brahma, the creator.

To celebrate Goddess Durga's triumph over the buffalo demon Mahisasura, Asta Matrika dancers perform in Patan's Mul Chowk. Men and boys dressed to represent the mother-earth goddesses become possessed with the goddesses energy and act out each gods characteristics. The act was initiated in the 17th century by the Malla King Srinivasa, whose father built the Krishna temple in Patan.

Indrani dances in an orange colored mask whose body is covered with eyes, nobody can hide from her. Maheswari, dances with a white mask; the female aspect of Shiva who continually combats the demons. Brahmayani, in a yellow mask is the human aspect of Brahma, the creator.

Dasain honors the goddess Durga—invested with the power of all the gods—and her victory over the terrible buffalo demon, Mahisasura. Durga demands blood sacrifice: tantric rites are carried out in the Taleju courtyard in Patan before slaughtering buffalo, the representation of Mahisasura. Men dressed in red from the khasai (butcher) caste perform the sacrifices; however, because these men use the kharga (sword), they are considered descendants of royalty. Legend

The eighth day of Dasain, Kal Ratri, "Black Night," begins a twenty-four-hour bloodbath to appease the goddess with the slaughter of an estimated ten thousand animals across the city. Simultaneously, Tibetan Buddhists at Swayambhu and Bodnath offer prayers and pujas for the souls of the dead animals. On the morning of the ninth day, the streets are quiet, but for occasional rifle volleys from the military. By the end of the day, every regiment of the Nepalese police and army, every owner of a plane, bus, car, machine and tool in the city, every family takes its share of blood. Chickens, ducks, and goats are ritually slaughtered on the engines of every vehicle, an assurance of safety for the coming year.

No flight of Nepal's national airline, RNAC, takes off until its engine is bathed in fresh blood. No worker feels safe using his tools until they are blessed by sacrifice.

The largest and most colorful ceremony takes place outside the old royal palace of Hanuman Dhoka at Kathmandu's Durbar Square, the same courtyard where Jung Bahadur Rana slaughtered all of his opponents in 1846. By mid morning the ceremony is in full swing beneath the bright sunshine. Clusters of golden flags, one for each regiment of the Nepalese army, are marked with bloody palmprints. A line of severed goat and buffalo heads sits below, among puja offer-

tells how Durga asked a Malla king to slaughter a buffalo for her. He replied that it would be impossible without a butcher. She commanded the king to search one out—specifically, to find a man who is defecating in the direction of the sun. The king's servants spotted a man doing just that and brought the subject before the king. It turned out to be the king's son. So, to this very day, the sacrificial executioners wear royal red and wield the mighty kharga.

Dasain not only honors the goddess Durga but also Ram and his conquest of the ten-headed demon, King Ravana of Sri Lanka. Many people believe that Ram spent nine days imbibing the shakti (female energy) power of Durga before he and the monkey god, Hanuman, attacked Ravana on the tenth day.

On the ninth day of Dasain, called Navami, in a military courtyard behind Hanuman Dhoka, soldiers carry out sacrifices in the spirit of the-more-you-can-the-more-you-gain. The sacrifice is also symbolic of slaying the animal part of one's self. Throughout this day, Nepalese perform the Vishwakarma ritual to honor the god of crafts and transport. Chicken, sheep, or goat blood is sprayed on tools and vehicles as a blessing.

182

ings of fruit, rice, flowers, pots of holy water, and burning lamps.

A military band strikes up a merry tune that sounds like circus music, and a black water buffalo is led, docile and willing, to one of the flag clusters. Other buffalo and goats stand placidly on the sidelines, despite the heady aroma of blood from a pile of nearby carcasses. An audience of dignitaries—all male—stands watching from within the courtyard. On a balcony above, a line of tourists stand with cameras poised.

The goddess Durga particularly likes the sacrifice of black male buffalo, a celebration of her defeat of a great demon buffalo in battle. This sacrificial animal is sprinkled with water and dips its head, a sign that it has accepted the sacrifice. A soldier hoists his sword. If the animal is not beheaded with one stroke, it is an ill omen, and the executioner is disgraced. Bang. The guns go off, the sword comes down, and the buffalo head falls to the earth. The death of the animal symbolizes the death of the bestial nature in human beings.

The band's gay tune resumes, and men dressed in white drag the animal carcass in a circle, marking the earth with its blood. The ritual continues, with an animal beheaded every two minutes, until five hundred have been slaughtered, later to provide a feast for the soldiers.

Most sacrifices are not so merciful as the quick sword blow of Hanuman Dhoka. Usually, the animal's throat is slit and held back while the blood spurts onto the object to be blessed. The higher the jet of blood rises, the more merit the sacrifice has.

SEASON OF HARVEST

Following rice harvest, villagers tie together bundles of rice stalks to be used for cooking fuel and livestock fodder.

All day, people hurry through the streets, bearing animal carcasses or animal heads on plates of puja offerings, or leading live animals toward temples for their turn on the sacrificial altar. At the end of the day, there is a feast in every home, and, on the final day of Dasain, families and friends wish each other well with tikka blessings, and long lines wait patiently outside the Royal Palace to receive the blessing of the king and queen.

In November yet another of the valley's calendars begins its new year, during the festival of Tihar, the Newari New Year.

Within two months, a blanket of fog covers the land each morning, and another year of timeless rituals begins anew in the Kathmandu Valley.

A Newari woman winnows rice, tipping a
nanglo into the wind.

Newari women work together winnowing rice.

On a fall morning in Kokonah, a Newari woman uses a bamboo nanglo to sweep rice chaff from a drying pile of unhusked rice.

189

Newari women from Godavari break apart clods of earth in preparation for winter wheat planting.

A Newari man urges his pair of oxen home
under a full moon.

Afterword

Doing a photographic book about the Kathmandu Valley was a daunting task and yet a dream come true. Having spent the last eleven years living in Nepal has given me considerable time to absorb the swirl of cultures and their traditions and to develop a comparative awareness that life is changing here with great speed, and that unless someone documents the traditions now, they will evolve into something quite different in less than a decade and be forgotten. Already many young Nepalese women have discarded saris for pants, and they have cut their once-braided hair to match the newest Western hairstyles. Rooftops once covered only with drying sliced pumpkin, chilies, and ears of corn now sport TV antennas as well.

Amid the change there remain the festivals; learn about them, and you'll come to understand the interplay between the gods and the Nepalese.

Photographing the Kathmandu Valley on any given day is like reading six different books at the same time. Work, rhythm, agricultural terrain, religious shrines, rituals, and ethnicity change within a fifteen-minute bicycle ride. Within a single hour, it is possible to sit along the Bagmati River watching a Hindu cremation, then circle Bodhanath's Buddhist stupa with hundreds of devout pilgrims.

To me, what is most special about the Kathmandu Valley is the opportunity to see integrated life. Take a minute to watch the swirling activity in Asan Tol's outdoor market. A lady will be selling a freshly plucked papaya, turn her head to catch a cow munching on her nearby lettuce pile, and, before slapping the cow's head, touch her hand to its head, then to her own—an automatic blessing.

Integrated tolerance is quintessentially Nepalese.

Focusing on the historical layers, the present, and the seasons, deserves three different books; yet, I hope, from this one you have gotten a feeling for all the separate realities that still exist today.

—THOMAS L. KELLY

Acknowledgments

I am greatly indebted to many people for their help and generosity in the creation of this book.

It all starts with His Majesty's Government of Nepal, which gave me permission to stay in the Kathmandu Valley long enough to document the four seasons.

Makunda Raj Aryal and Major General Aditya Shumsher J. B. Rana provided invaluable introductions to the Patan City artisans and furnished information concerning local legend. The historical Rana photographs were obtained through the generosity of General Narayan Shumsher Rana and Kiran and Triloky Chitrakar. The companionship and help of my photographic assistant, Durga Pathak, contributed much pleasure to the process of making the book.

I owe special thanks to my parents, Bud and Jeanne Kelly, sister Susan, and even more to my brother, Robert, for their inspiration and devoted support.

Lastly, my deepest thanks go to Carroll Dunham for her picture editing and editorial opinions, but more importantly for her confidence, patience, and companionship.

—TLK

INDEX

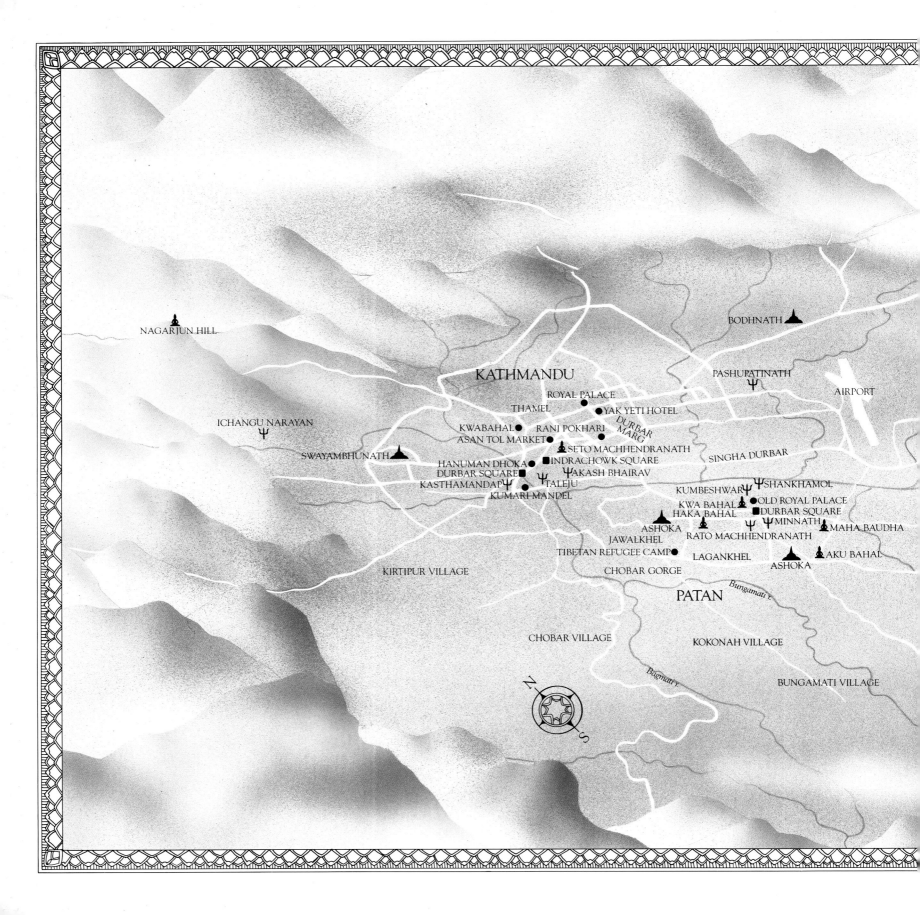

NAGARJUN HILL

BODHNATH

KATHMANDU

PASHUPATINATH

ROYAL PALACE

AIRPORT

THAMEL

YAK YETI HOTEL

ICHANGU NARAYAN

KWABAHAL

RANI POKHARI

DURBAR MARG

ASAN TOL MARKET

SWAYAMBHUNATH

SETO MACHHENDRANATH

SINGHA DURBAR

HANUMAN DHOKA

INDRACHOWK SQUARE

DURBAR SQUARE

AKASH BHAIRAV

KUMBESHWAR

SHANKHAMOL

KASTHAMANDAP

TALEJU

KWA BAHAL

OLD ROYAL PALACE

KUMARI MANDEL

HAKA BAHAL

DURBAR SQUARE

MINNATH

MAHA BAUDHA

ASHOKA

JAWALKHEL

RATO MACHHENDRANATH

TIBETAN REFUGEE CAMP

LAGANKHEL

ASHOKA

AKU BAHAL

KIRTIPUR VILLAGE

CHOBAR GORGE

Bungamati r.

PATAN

CHOBAR VILLAGE

KOKONAH VILLAGE

Bagmati r.

BUNGAMATI VILLAGE

N

S